Contemporary Worship

in the Reformed Tradition

Practical Approaches for Congregations

DAVID A. MILLER

VITAL FAITH RESOURCES

ISBN **1-931551-00-6**

VITAL FAITH RESOURCES
PO Box 18378
Pittsburgh, PA 15236

Telephone 412-655-4958

ACKNOWLEDGMENTS

This book could never have been produced without the love and support of so many of my friends and family. In particular, I would like to thank the following people.

To my wife, Leslie: Your constant encouragement and willingness to sacrifice made this book possible. Once again I can see why God chose you to be my helpmate, and I am so grateful for your love and commitment to me.

To my three precious children, Christy, Daniel, and Laura: Thank you for sharing your daddy in allowing him to finish this book.

To my faithful friend and secretary, Sally Otten: Thank you for your typing, editing, and genuine excitement about this book and how it can help other churches.

To my proofreading team – Cathy Crelin, Fran Darling, Gloria Hecker, Mindy La Grande, Sara Miller, Elizabeth Small, Pat Wall, and Karen Young: Your efforts have helped me express my ideas more clearly and accurately.

To my brother Pat: Your love and practical support have made all the difference!

To my Faith Presbyterian Church congregation: Thank you for your many expressions of support and encouragement. You have played a very real part in helping me struggle to understand and refine many of the ideas set forth in the following pages.

To all of the pastors who participated in the case studies: Thank you for the thoughtful and honest commentary that you provided for the case studies. I feel that with each one of you, I have found a new friend and colleague in ministry. I praise God for your courage and willingness to provide such vital leadership to your churches in the area of worship. The worship life of your congregations has truly become a beacon of hope for other churches.

TABLE OF CONTENTS

INTRODUCTION

In *Room for God?* author Robert Wenz tells the following story of something that took place in a church in the Los Angeles area:

> It was the first Sunday of the summer...The senior pastor had arranged to have a worship team lead the service to put a "spark" into the otherwise depressed summer vacation season. The worship team moved the pulpit aside, rolled the baby grand piano to the center of the large platform, plugged in an electric keyboard, and focused their overhead projector. As the service began, the words of the choruses ... were projected on the screen. Some songs were new to the congregation, some better known. The service was less formal than that of Sundays past, but the music barely approached one-tenth the volume of a Michael W. Smith concert – no drums, no ten-foot-high speaker columns. Many worshippers seemed to enjoy the new format. Others remained politely stoic. Little could the pastor have anticipated the size of the blast his "spark" would ignite. It would come to be measured in megatons. Following the service, several members of the congregation stormed the platform to denounce the "debauchery" to which they had been reluctant witnesses. Sound-system operators threw down their keys and walked out in protest. One saint spat on the floor in disgust and threatened never to return. The church was thrown into turmoil. The explosion started a series of California-style brush fires that have yet to be "knocked down."[1]

I believe that in most churches we can avoid this kind of painful, destructive conflict *if* we focus both on what the Bible teaches about worship and on the best of Reformed tradition. Contemporary worship *can* be done with theological integrity, musical excellence, and cultural relevance.

I passionately hope as you take this journey with me, you will discover insights that you can adapt to your unique context. Having introduced contemporary worship in two different Presbyterian churches, I know the agony and ecstasy that go with this territory. I hope this study of the lessons learned by myself and others who have gone before you will help you introduce change in a sensitive, inclusive, and strategic way.

If your church is contemplating starting a contemporary service, you might be tempted to turn to the more practical *how to* sections found in Chapters 4 and 5. I urge you not to rush past the first three chapters, which lay a theological foundation for all that follows. Growth in worship flows not from the right technique, but from the right understanding of who God is and why we should worship God. Out of this understanding, each of us can craft worship in a way that fits the needs of our particular congregation. As the adage goes, "There is nothing so practical as a theory that is true."

Other voices in the church oppose the approach I have taken, and any serious consideration of contemporary worship must address these concerns. To keep a positive, uninterrupted focus for those who are most interested in starting a contemporary worship service, I have set forth the theology, design, and practice of contemporary worship in this book. For those who want an in-depth theological discussion of all the issues and controversies surrounding this subject, the bibliography suggests further reading.

Every strategic plan will eventually meet with some resistance. Do not lose heart: The benefits far outweigh the cost involved in starting contemporary worship. Sunday morning continues to be the most strategic hour in the week for both nurture and outreach. Launching a contemporary worship service can dramatically affect the church's outreach. The more we enrich our worship, the more we will bring renewal to our congregations. Vibrant worship leads to a growing and dynamic church. I hope this book will assist pastors, worship committees, and all others in leading the church effectively and with joy. Questions at the end of each chapter are designed to facilitate discussion and planning. May you and your congregation be challenged to worship God in new and deeper ways, and thus be able to "sing a new song for joy to the Lord" (Psalm 33:3, paraphrased).

Music to Tell
The Good News

Let the Earth Hear His Voice

The church took its first breath on the Day of Pentecost when the Holy Spirit moved with power among Jews who had come to Jerusalem from many places, speaking many languages. All the Jewish pilgrims understood the message of God's Spirit, and each one could say, "In our own languages we hear them speaking about God's deeds of power" (Acts 2:11). Across the centuries, whenever we find new breath or renewal in the Church, we can trace it to this simple truth: God's word has been spoken in new ways, in the language of the people, in a way that demonstrates its relevance to the contemporary culture. The Apostle Paul adapted his words to his surrounding culture so that he could communicate the Gospel in a relevant way: "To the weak I became weak, so that I might win the weak. I have become all things to all people, that I might by all means save some. I do it all for the sake of the gospel, so that I may share in its blessings" (1 Corinthians 9:22-23). At times this meant stretching beyond comfortable patterns for Paul. Given the decadent and even barbaric first-century Gentile moral climate (especially Corinth!), Paul could have urged Christians to avoid any association with pagan culture. Yet Paul in God's love sought not to abandon culture, but rather to redeem it. For Paul the *message* was sacred, but the *methods* by which it was conveyed were shaped by the culture of those he labored to reach. Paul employed all possible means to win others to faith in Christ. In today's culture Paul might say, "To the baby boomers, I become as a baby boomer; to seniors, I become as a senior; to the rock and rollers, I become as a rock and roller."

Paul adapted his message to the language and customs of a culture because he distinguished cultural style from theological content. This implies that many cultural forms are morally neutral. They can convey the values of the kingdom of darkness or the values of the Kingdom of God. We can employ various aspects of culture to serve God's purpose because "Christ is the transformer of culture."[1]

Following Paul's example, we must communicate God's love and truth in appropriate and relevant ways to our surrounding culture. Typically we realize this more clearly when we talk about foreign missions. It would not occur to us to begin mission work with a primitive tribe by first insisting the natives learn English! No, we go to them, learn their language, understand their culture. Language, music, dress, art, and social customs also are part of the cultural tapestry. When it comes to sharing God's Word, music provides a key. Our world welcomes an astonishing variety of musical sounds. The sounds of a sitar may appeal to a person from Asia, while someone from Africa may enjoy a different rhythm and tone. The Middle Eastern ear may be drawn to a different scale and sound. Only cultural elitism suggests that one solitary style of music truly represents *sacred music.*

If infused with the truth of the Gospel, a world of musical styles can serve a sacred purpose and bring glory to God in worship. At Pentecost, God blew the lid off the just-for-us box and unleashed the power of the Gospel to everyone in a multitude of languages so that each could understand. Our charge is the same, to spread the Gospel to all whether they are far away or in the neighborhood.

Who Is Your Audience?

We can broaden our outreach if we broaden our musical repertory. Musical style, more than almost any other human factor, determines whom the church will reach. Rick Warren, a noted pastor and author in the area of church growth, asserts, "If you were to tell me the kind of music you are currently using in your services, I could describe the kind of people you are reaching without even visiting your church. I could also tell you the kind of people your church will never be able to reach."[2] Contemporary music appeals to a broad range of people, but by far the largest group that embraces this style is the generation often referred to as the baby boomers.[3] At this writing nearly 30 percent of the population fall into this group, born between 1946 and 1964. Just behind them, born between 1965 and 1983 and often dubbed the "baby busters," the next demographic group in America measures just over 26 percent of the total. Their children account for about 16 percent of the population. Older than 53 years of age? Just over a quarter of Americans have passed this point. The point is that more than half of our nation's population is made up of boomers and busters. Can the Church connect with the baby boomers and their children and grandchildren? It will require some effort for our "graying church" to reach them.

The following chart suggests the boomer generation represents a very ripe mission field. More than half of the boomers in the United States do not participate in any church.

Most baby boomers remember what church was like. Many of their friends never left the church. Even though many boomers have left the church, they have not necessarily stopped believing. One study noted, "More than 80 percent of the boomers consider themselves religious and believe in life after death."[5]

The Spiritual Formation of the Boomer Generation[4]

75-80 percent	exposed to Sunday school and youth ministries
33 percent	never left the church
50-60 percent	dropped out
33 percent	returned to church in the past 5 years
over 50 percent	minimized participation or dropped out

When baby boomers do come back to a church, it seems "a little child shall lead them." About 60 percent of the boomers who return to church are married with children.[6] Boomers and busters who are rearing children more rapidly welcome morals and values to help them raise a family. Author Donald M. Brandt notes how these demographics present a unique outreach opportunity for the Church:

> From a mission orientation, this generation presents a marvelous opportunity. Counting their children, baby boomers and their families make up the majority of U.S. residents. Add to this the "baby busters" (those born between 1965 and 1976) and *their* children, and we are dealing with close to two-thirds of the American population. The baby boomer nesting stage is winding down—and rapidly. The busters now beginning their nesting stage—are a much smaller group. Once the boomers have moved on to their next life stage, it will be far more difficult for churches to reach either boomers or their children. In other words this is a "for a-limited-time-only" opportunity.[7]

The good news is that many churches are reaching baby boomers by offering solid and significant ministry to children, along with a contemporary music style in worship. Some experts call the return of the baby boomers to church "a baby boomerang." Herb Miller notes that the top three reasons for choosing a church have changed considerably. In the past people chose a church because of its "doctrine, denomination, family tradition."[8] Today people choose a church for worship style, quality of ministries, and warmth and caring. Miller says, "Seventy percent of young adults with birth dates after 1946 find this style of worship (contemporary or alternative style) more spiritually meaningful."[9]

Sadly, mainline churches in the United States often miss out on this ministry opportunity. Eric Snyder argues persuasively that the decline of the Presbyterian Church (USA) is related to its inability to reach baby boomers. The traditional style of worship often employed in the mainline denominations frequently represents something negative to baby boomers. Robes, pews, organs, and stated liturgy smack of a dry formalism they associate with an irrelevant religion.[10] On the other hand, when many of these same people walk into a congregation that has a pulsating beat and relevant, fresh language, they respond with new interest. Robert Logan describes the reaction of someone who discovers contemporary worship: "For the first time in my life, I'm enjoying and looking forward to coming to church. I feel so comfortable. I love the music! For the first time in a church I feel I can get close to God."[11] Herb Miller writes, "Young adults who did not grow up in the church are more energized when they visit a contemporary service and more likely to return the following week."[12]

Contemporary music, despite its key role, is but one dimension of contemporary worship. Other aspects of culture also affect our worship style. These include our language, dress, symbols, visual aids, and the architecture of the sanctuary. Daniel C. Benedict and Craig Kennet Miller offer the following definition for contemporary worship:

> A movement and a style of worship that focuses on the culturally accessible and relevant, on the new and innovative, on the use of recent technologies of communication for the purpose of outreach to seekers and those who are disenchanted with more traditional styles of worship.[13]

The defining feature of contemporary worship has more to do with the style of worship than the content of worship. A church may have a biblical understanding of worship but maintain a culturally irrelevant style. Further, it is possible to have deficient understanding of biblical worship with a style that is contemporary. Given the graying of mainline Christian churches and the appeal of contemporary worship, it is time to ask the hard question: Can we preserve what is meaningful and valued in our church while at the same time broadening our style of worship to minister more effectively to all generations? I believe we can. I believe we must.

Listen to the Music

Much of the baby boomer culture is shaped around music – often called contemporary music. The dictionary defines "contemporary" simply as "with the times." We recognize today's pop culture music by its strong and steady beat; simple, short music structure; frequent use of syncopated rhythms; the importance of flow (segues between songs using improvisation and modulation); and the use of guitars and electronic instruments (synthesizer and MIDI sequencers).

Tune in to an FM radio station and listen to one station after another. The vast majority of stations will play what we know as adult, middle-of-the-road contemporary music. It has become the predominant musical form, not only in our culture, but also across the world.

Music Is Controversial

People forge fierce loyalties to their style of music. In *Room for God?* Robert Wenz makes the following observation:

> Thousands of churches in the United States are at some point along the continuum between debate and destruction over the issue of what is the right kind of worship to offer God. The debate has become not only as intense and divisive as in the Pro-Choice/Pro-Life debate in the American political arena, but it also seems to have become an emotional debate that ignores the available biblical instruction.[14]

This debate intensifies because we have fused – and confused – our worship style and theology. Some faithful churchgoers take offense if we sing the words from a favorite hymn to a more contemporary musical arrangement. It is easier to change the theology of the church than it is to change the style of music! Even the smallest of changes in a traditional worship service can evoke strong and negative reaction. Rick Warren writes, "Music is a divisive issue that separates generations, regions of the country, personality types, and even family members. So we should not be surprised when opinions on music differ in the church."[15]

Often the division caused by music exposes the generation gap in the church. I recall a conversation that took place after a "Youth Sunday" in a church where the worship style was mostly traditional. The Youth Director was standing at the door, greeting people as they left the sanctuary. An older member of the church remarked, "Well, I'm glad we got that over with, and I'm also glad we only have to do this once a year." The Youth Director responded, "Well, maybe now you know how the young people feel about the other fifty-one Sundays during the year!"

Let's try to "de-emotionalize" the debate by affirming the validity of a variety of styles. We will insist that the crucial question is not "What is the proper style of worship?" but "What is the proper content of worship?"

Music Is Powerful

Aristotle once said, "Music has the power to shape character."[16] Music can stir our emotions. When those emotions connect to the things we believe, our beliefs gain strength and depth. Pioneers of faith speak to the importance of music in worship. John Calvin put it this way, "Music has a very powerful tendency to stir up the mind to true zeal and ardor."[17] Martin Luther writes:

> My heart bubbles up and overflows in response to music... Music is to be praised as second only to the word of God because by her all the emotions are swayed . . . This precious gift has been bestowed on men alone to remind them that they are created to praise and magnify the Lord.[18]

Sally Morgenthaler expresses a similar thought: "Aside from the Spirit of God, music is the most potent element in a worship service. It has an incredible, matchless capacity to open the human heart to God, accessing the soul more quickly, deeply, and permanently than any other art form or human speech."[19] Music can fire the heart, but music can also extinguish spiritual passion.

When I have preached in churches with two services, I have noticed how the worship style can affect how we hear God's Word. When there is a time of vibrant and heartfelt singing, I can sense an eagerness for the preached Word. On the other hand, if the singing is half-hearted and perfunctory, the sermon feels like an uphill battle. In one service, the message finds welcome; in the other, it falls flat and makes little impact. The difference is in the worship!

Music Is a Disputable Matter

In Romans 14, Paul deals with controversies like clean and unclean foods, which day should be holy, and what kind of drink was forbidden (Romans 14:2, 5, 21). Paul calls these controversies "disputable matters." They are "disputable" in that Christians can act with good conscience and still honestly disagree.[20] Because these issues touch no essential point of the Gospel, we classify them as having secondary theological significance. Paul's counsel first affirms our unity in Christ. God calls us to bear with one another and "pursue what makes for peace and for mutual upbuilding" (Romans 14:19) when dealing with the disputable matter. The "weaker brother" is the one who takes the more restrictive view, seeing good things in God's creation, such as food and drink, as "unclean" because of their association with evil (Romans 14:14).

The Scriptures portray music as one of God's good gifts in creation. Like language, music can be experienced in a great variety. In Paul's day some Jews felt that eating certain kinds of meat would defile them. Today some Christians look at some forms of contemporary music as inherently evil. Some even teach that the "rock beat" is of the devil. But those who have studied the history of music know that the devil has dabbled with more than just rock music. Graham Cray points out: "There's probably no musical form in existence, which within its original context, does not send some messages which are in conflict with the Christian message."[21]

Yet the differences that divide us over music have little or nothing to do with biblical essentials; they relate more to cultural and generational preferences. The weaker brother or sister passes judgment on others who embrace a different style of music. If we substitute the word "music" for "food," Paul's counsel becomes very relevant: "I know and am persuaded in the Lord Jesus that *no music* is unclean in itself" (Romans 14:14). Consider these points noted by Barry Liesch:

> Harps were guitars, small and portable, in the Old Testament. Asaph, David's chief musician, was a percussionist. Puritans in England took axes to organs, sang no hymns (only scriptural psalms), and prohibited instruments in worship. In 1903 the Pope banned the piano as a secular instrument unfit for public worship.[22]

To help us work through the problem of disputable matters, Paul gives the following advice:

Live together in the differences (Romans 15:1).
Both the traditionalist and the avant-garde belong in the Church.

Process the differences in love (Romans 14:15).
Do not condemn, but rather accommodate when possible.

Nurture the church to be "strong."
Lay down theological principles that will help people see that "nothing is unclean in itself" (Romans 14:14).

Develop core values that promote "righteousness and peace and joy in the Holy Spirit" (Romans 14:17).

Move forward in a way that will best promote the unity, peace, and spiritual growth of the church (Romans 14:19).

Music Is Constantly Changing
Many of the traditional hymns in the Church today were once considered *too contemporary!* Those who protest singing "secular music" may be surprised to learn the origin of some of their favorite

sacred hymns. John Wesley was known in his day for going out among the people to preach the Gospel. He found that people were very willing to listen to his message but unenthusiastic about the songs. John commissioned his brother Charles to write music that common people could eagerly embrace. Charles wrote these songs for evangelistic purposes and never intended them for services in the church. His *O for a Thousand Tongues to Sing* was deemed, in its day, *too contemporary* for church services. Now it is considered a hallmark of "sacred" music.[23] We sing Martin Luther's classic hymn *A Mighty Fortress Is Our God* to a tune borrowed from the beer gardens of Luther's day. The same music that can express trivial or even vulgar words can also be used as a vehicle for great spiritual blessing. The question is not "Will we sing secular music?" Rather, it is "Which secular music? The secular music of past generations or the secular music of today?"[24]

Around the globe and across the centuries, disciples bring new music into the church. Eventually the new song becomes a part of the sacred tradition. What we ban as profane today may well end up in our grandchildren's hymnbooks!

Music Is a Unique Kind of Language

Benedict and Miller, in their excellent book *Contemporary Worship for the Twenty-first Century*, describe music as a language of the heart.

> You have undoubtedly observed persons for whom English was a second language break into their "native tongue." Their speech just poured out. It was animated and clearly a release of natural energy that was not evident when speaking the "foreign" language. It was their language of the heart. The language in which their emotions could flow along with cognitive expression . . . Music and language that do not recognize and release worshipers to hear and express themselves in the heart-language fail to recognize them . . . you will need to find ways to plan and lead worship that are impressive and expressive in the heart-language and heart-music of the eth-

nic, generational, or subculture groups whose participation you invite.[25] music also promotes awareness, is prophetic, expands and challenges.

Dan Gilbert, a Lutheran pastor, described how a missionary came to understand the heart-language of the people he ministered to in Nigeria:

When he [former Lutheran missionary Ed Rupprecht] was first in Nigeria in the 1960's, the missionaries taught the people to sing traditional Western hymn melodies with words in the local language. When Ed and his wife, Wilma, were married in Nigeria, the people asked if they could compose their own worship song for the wedding. Permission was granted, and the song was composed and offered up in the worship of the one, true God. Afterwards, one of the local men said to Ed something like, 'Can we do this more often? We can't beat our drums to your music.' We may be tempted to smile patronizingly, 'Oh, how cute.' But, O how excellent it is when people praise the Lord with the expressions of their heart. Only pride would prompt a person to say that a certain form of Western music is somehow more pleasing or superior in any way.[26]

Many of the baby boomers who have come back into the church are saying today, "We cannot beat our drums to your music." Some of them will stay in the church and continue to speak a foreign musical language. Others will get lost in the translation. We can overcome this language barrier if we will broaden our style of worship to include the younger generations. We can overcome it if we are willing to follow the example of Paul and invite people to respond to Christ and not the culture and language of the one who bears the message. Benedict and Miller suggest we explore whether existing services might be broadened to sound in several heart-languages so a broader range of persons hears and sings in their heart-language, or whether we might offer several services so that people have

11

options that make worship culturally accessible.[27]

One recent study indicated that classical music accounts for only 2 percent of the record sales in America, yet in many churches the classical music style accounts for 98 percent of the music![28] When we adopt a cultural style as the basis of our worship, we open ourselves to a form of pride that insists "the music that helps me to experience a closeness to God is superior to all other styles." In his essay "Music in Service to the Gospel" Richard Armstrong notes:

> To speak of good music in contrast to bad music presupposes some kind of standard by which to assess its value and qualities. But who sets the standards? Are not the standards themselves culturally conditioned? Obviously they are. I know a teacher and choral conductor who argues that the familiar tune to *Beneath the Cross of Jesus* is not good music. But that does not keep it from being one of my favorite hymn tunes.[29]

Missionary Alan Tippett, drawing upon a lesson from history, reminds us of the negative consequences that will result from pride and ethnocentrism:

> In the 1840's missionaries to the Fiji Islands paraphrased Charles Wesley's lyrics into Fijian and invited the native people to chant these words in their own scales and idioms. The project was a spectacular success. Forty years later a new group of missionaries arrived and insisted that the old rhythms and tunes be sung exactly as notated in their English hymn books. This new construction was never well received; the tunes and rhythms felt strange to the people.[30]

Many critics of contemporary music in the church seem to imply that the modern music has been "tainted" by culture, whereas the great hymns of the church were wrapped up in a grand, mysterious package and let down from heaven on a string. As we have seen, most church music traces its roots in secular culture. Music's acceptability has more to do with the cultural heart-language than with the inherent beauty or spirituality of the music. A pulsating rock beat may, for some, signal jubilant celebration. For others it is distracting, incoherent racket.

If we confuse our cultural style with our theology, contemporary worship appears to be a departure from a holy tradition. One Episcopal priest put it this way, "For us, our form is our essence."[31] Marva Dawn, a leading critic of contemporary worship, argues that those who prefer contemporary worship might embrace traditional worship if it were explained in a relevant way. She writes, "The major reason why tradition often grows stale is that we have failed to educate worshipers to know why we do what we do and who we are as a worshiping community carrying the faith together."[32]

Can instruction change someone's heart-song? I am reminded of an elder in a Presbyterian church who once confessed that, even though he was well schooled in Presbyterian traditions, he found himself "sneaking" over to a local Community Church for an early service that featured contemporary music. Later he would attend the more formal service at his own church. In his own tradition he found safety and familiarity. In the Community Church he found a worship style that resonated with his "native musical tongue."

God in His wisdom has given us principles and not prescriptions for worship. If we desire worship services that are meaningful for everyone in our church and in the broader community, we must not only enrich the old style, but also enable worship in the heart-songs of all people. Chuck Fromm of Maranatha Music sounds this warning: "We better think about sound and how we are reaching our community or we will be the Amish of the twenty-first century."[33]

Questions for Discussion

1. What is your favorite radio station?
2. Does it play a different style of music than the style of music in your church?
3. What does this tell you about worship?

4. Agree or disagree? The message is sacred but the methods by which we communicate that message will vary, depending on whom we're trying to reach.
5. Is there really one sacred music style?
6. If we did a survey among our congregation, which style of music would they say they prefer?
7. What are the implications of this for music in worship?
8. What style of music do people in our community who do not attend our church prefer?
9. What implications does this have for designing worship services?

Note: The "Directory for Worship" for the Presbyterian Church (USA) offers rich insight on this point. If we understand music to be a kind of heart-language, the section that addresses appropriate language for church becomes very relevant:

> Appropriate language seeks to recognize the variety of traditions which reflect the biblical truth authentically in their own forms of speech and action. In doing so the church honors and properly uses the language of the tradition. The church is nonetheless free to be innovative in seeking appropriate language for worship. While respecting time-honored forms and set orders, the church may reshape them to respond freely to the leading of God's Spirit in every age. Since the Presbyterian Church USA is a family of peoples united in Jesus Christ, appropriate language for its worship should display the rich variety of these people. To the extent that forms, actions, languages, or settings of worship exclude the expression of diverse culture represented in the church, or deny emerging needs and identities of believers, that worship is not faithful to the life, death and resurrection of Jesus Christ (W-1.2005 and W-1.20060).[34]

The Essentials of Worship

2

Contemporary worship and traditional worship differ in style, not in substance. Whenever we worship God "in spirit and in truth," our worship is authentic and pleasing to God. Let's consider how this understanding can bring unity amid diversity of styles.

When Jesus encountered the woman at the well, they talked about worship. Jesus made it clear that not every worship experience is equally valid. He told the woman, "But the hour is coming . . . when true worshipers will worship the Father in spirit and truth, for the Father seeks such as these to worship him" (John 4:23). Here Jesus describes the essence of worship: spirit and truth.

Worship "in spirit" will be sincere and wholehearted. In Romans 12:1, Paul invites us to this kind of worship when he urges us to present our "bodies as a living sacrifice, holy and acceptable to God, which is your *spiritual worship*" (italics mine). Jesus defines worship "in truth" in John 17. As he prays in the garden of Gethsemane for his disciples, he affirms, "Your word is truth" (John 17:17). The Scripture is our only certain guide for knowing whether our worship is connecting with the heart of God. Examine with me the Scriptural basis of authentic and God-pleasing worship.

Hebrews 11:6 describes how to draw near to God. "And without

5

faith it is impossible to please God, for whoever would approach him must believe that he exists and that he rewards those who seek him." Worship does not necessarily happen when we sing songs about God, nor even when we hear words spoken about God. Sally Morgenthaler has well observed that worship is not "just a roomful of people thinking inspired thoughts."[1] Worship begins when we believe that God is truly present and that He delights in filling a heart that is diligently seeking to find Him.

The great surprise of faith is this: *In seeking, we are found.* Even the very desire for God is a measure of God's grace to us. This is why Jesus said, "No one can come to me unless drawn by the Father who sent me" (John 6:44). This is humbling because we deserve no special honor for our worship of God, but at the same time it lifts us out of any sense of unworthiness. Our very thirst and hunger for God announce that God desires to meet us in worship.

God's grace draws us into worship and sustains us in our worship. Jesus Christ is the object of our worship and the mediator of our worship. It is Christ who leads his people to the throne of grace. These words by James Torrance are well worth pondering:

> This is the "wonderful exchange" (*mirifica commutatioa – commercium admirabile*) by which Christ takes what is ours (our broken lives and unworthy prayers), sanctifies them, offers them without spot or wrinkle to the Father, and gives them back to us, that we might "feed" upon him in thanksgiving. He takes our prayers and makes them his prayers, and he makes his prayers our prayers, and we know our prayers are heard "for Jesus' sake." This is life in the Spirit, worship understood in terms of *sola gratia* . . . With inward peace we are lifted up by the Spirit into the presence of the Father, into a life of wonderful communion, into a life of praise and adoration in union with Christ. We know that the living Christ is in our midst, leading our worship, our prayers and our praises.[2]

Scripture shows us a discernable pattern that characterizes this

grace-filled encounter with God. I have found the simple acrostic –
ACTS – a helpful way to recall it. Let's look at an excellent example
of this pattern for worship in Isaiah 6. The prophet Isaiah has a
vision of God, which leads him into worship. We read, "In the year
that King Uzziah died, I saw the LORD sitting on a throne, high and
lofty; and the hem of his robe filled the temple" (Isaiah 6:1). Isaiah's
worship begins with A – adoration.

The majesty of God fills us with awe, mystery, and wonder just
as Isaiah experienced this sense of awe when he caught a glimpse of
God as the exalted King of Heaven. At the heart of worship is a
vision of God as high and exalted. To praise God is to prize God!
Praise exalts God as our highest value. The English word *worship*
comes from the Old English word *worthscipe* that means *to ascribe
worth*. In worship we acknowledge, "God, you are worthy of my
honor. You are worthy to be praised for who you are and for all that
you have done. You are worth more to me than all the things of
earth."

Isaiah's adoration gives way to C – confession. He sees six-winged
seraphs singing, "Holy, holy, holy is the Lord of hosts; the whole
earth is full of his glory" (Isaiah 6:3). Isaiah sees the Lord as perfect
love, goodness, truth, and justice. Then in contrast, he recognizes his
own unworthiness. He cries out, "Woe is me! I am lost, for I am a
man of unclean lips, and I live among a people of unclean lips"
(Isaiah 6:5).

When Isaiah encounters the holiness of God, he says, "I am
ruined." He no longer sees himself as God's righteous prophet con-
demning the sins of others. The holiness of God shatters Isaiah's self-
righteousness. Isaiah's response is typical of people in the Bible who
encounter a sense of God's holiness. Peter, with Jesus beside him,
took in a miraculous catch of fish. Peter's response was to fall down
before Christ and say, "Go away from me, Lord, for I am a sinful
man!" (Luke 5:8). When the Apostle John caught a vision of the res-
urrected Christ, he fell down as if he were dead (Revelation 1:17).
Before Paul met Christ, he could describe himself as a Pharisee of the

Pharisees, but after his Damascus Road experience, he described himself as the "chief of sinners" (1 Timothy 1:15).

Even though we may want to deny it, the reality is that our lives fall far short of God's holy standard. Against the straight edge of God's holiness, our crooked ways become apparent. Martin Luther once said, "The first rule of prayer is don't lie to God."[3] In confession we encounter a God who judges us with love. Søren Kierkegaard wrote of the connection between grace and confession with the following prayer:

> Father in heaven! Hold not our sins up against us but hold us up against our sins, so that the thought of Thee, when it wakens, should not remind us of what we have committed but of what thou didst forgive, not of how we went astray but of how thou didst save us.[4]

Confession leads us toward T – thanksgiving. Isaiah's vision moves from the throne to the altar, the place of sacrifice. From the altar, a seraph takes a burning coal, touches Isaiah's lips with it and says to him, "Now that this has touched your lips, your guilt has departed and your sin is blotted out" (Isaiah 6:7).

In John's gospel we discover that the one Isaiah saw on the throne was in fact our Lord Jesus Christ. John writes, "Isaiah said this because he saw Jesus' glory and spoke about him" (John 12:41, NIV). The high and exalted One was the preincarnate Word, who was "with God" and "was God" from all eternity (John 1:1). Jesus is the "Lamb of God who takes away the sin of the world," slain on the altar for us (John 1:29). Even though we were not worthy, the sacrifice of this Lamb has removed our guilt and "blotted out" our sin. The seraph then touches Isaiah's lips with the burning coal. It is painful because it is not easy to give up the idols of our hearts, but it also brings an instant and complete purging of Isaiah's sins.

Such an experience of God's grace can only lead our hearts to thanksgiving and praise. Like David of old we can say, "He put a new song in my mouth, a song of praise to our God" (Psalm 40:3).

Because of what Christ has done for us, we can "enter his gates with thanksgiving, and his courts with praise" (Psalm 100:4). Here is a cause for celebration and joy in worship. In adoration, we acknowledge the greatness of God's love. In confession, even the memory of sin leads us toward God's grace. In thanksgiving and praise, we acknowledge God's goodness and grace.

The majesty and grace of God move our hearts toward S – supplication. This is a word that is not heard often in the church. Here it is used to mean earnest prayer for ourselves and others. Psalm 51 shows us this connection. David moves from confession to humble contrition (Psalm 51:17). He then offers prayers of supplication for Israel, "Do good to Zion in your good pleasure; rebuild the walls of Jerusalem" (Psalm 51:18). As we experience God's forgiveness, we are moved to cry out, "God of grace and God of glory, on Thy people pour Thy power."[5] We cry out to God afresh to free us from our anxiety, strengthen us, heal us in our pain, and guide us in those areas where we are uncertain. We pray throughout a worship service as we encounter God through reading the Scripture, preaching, and song. In the pastoral prayer we unite our hearts to pray specifically for the needs of God's people.

When we experience this ACTS pattern in worship our hearts are opened to God's Word. As God's Word is read and its meaning is opened to us, we hear God whispering in our hearts. The Day of Pentecost reveals this powerful relationship between worship and the preaching of the Word. Jews who were gathered from many nations in Jerusalem heard the Christians "declaring the wonders of God in our own tongues" (Acts 2:11, NIV). When they had witnessed this powerful movement of God's Spirit, we read, "Amazed and perplexed, they asked one another, 'What does this mean?' " (Acts 2:12, NIV). Peter then preaches his sermon, and the people "were cut to the heart" (Acts 2:37, NIV). Three thousand people became disciples of Christ (Acts 2:41). The preaching of the word helps us understand and respond to God. The prophet Isaiah refers to God's Word in this way: "It will not return to me empty, but will accomplish what I desire and achieve the purpose for which I sent it" (Isaiah 55:11, NIV). Notice that God has not promised to bless our preaching; he has promised to bless His Word. Preaching should set forth the word of God so that we can know God's purpose and experience his presence more fully. The sermon should lead people into an encounter with the living God who quickens our conscience, illumines our minds, and empowers our will to obey his Word.

In *Teaching a Stone to Talk*, Annie Dillard questions whether we really are in touch with the power of God in worship:

> The churches are children playing on the floor with their chemistry sets, mixing up a batch of TNT to kill a Sunday morning. It is madness to wear ladies' straw hats and velvet hats to church; we should all be wearing crash helmets. Ushers should issue life preservers and signal flares; they should lash us to our pews. For the sleeping god may wake someday and take offense, or the waking god may draw us out to where we can never return.[6]

As we meet God in worship, we will discover places in our lives that we must fully yield to God and dedicate to him. Return to the story of Isaiah. After the seraph touches Isaiah's lips, he hears the Lord saying, "Whom shall I send, and who will go for us?" (Isaiah 6:8 NIV). Before, Isaiah was overcome with a sense of his inadequacy in the presence of God. Now, knowing God's grace, he boldly responds, "Here am I; send me!" (Isaiah 6:8). Here is the dynamic connection between worship and service. To worship is to exalt Jesus Christ, to honor him as Lord of everything in our lives. If our desire is to please God, everything we do can be an act of worship. It does not matter whether we are eating an apple or building a bridge, word processing, or interacting with people. If it is done "as unto the Lord," it is worship.

Baptism and the Lord's Supper express our response to God. When we receive the sign of the covenant in baptism, we are declaring our allegiance to God. We publicly affirm that the decision to follow Christ is not something we do only in the privacy of our heart, but it is a decision to live as Christ's disciple in every area of life. Baptism symbolizes that we embrace a whole new life. Paul says, "Therefore we have been buried with him by baptism into death, so that, just as Christ was raised from the dead by the glory of the Father, so we too might walk in newness of life" (Romans 6:4). The Lord's Supper gives us the continual nourishment we need to live this new life. Receiving the bread and cup, we take into ourselves God's mercy and grace for the sins that weigh heavily upon our conscience. As we focus on our Savior's sacrifice, we remember that the pierced hand is the same hand that will gently guide our lives.

Another way we respond to God is through the giving of our tithes and offerings. We relinquish the possessions that have a special hold on our lives, turning away from the idolatry of things and worshiping God alone. In a concrete and tangible way, we show that we value God more than the material possessions and pleasures of this world. Like Isaiah we say, "Here am I, Lord. Everything I am and all I have is yours."

The benediction gives a charge to God's people to continue to honor Christ as Lord, not only in church, but also in everything they do. Someone has said, *"When the worship is over, let the service begin!"*

Assembling the Building Blocks

Once we have identified from scripture the essential building blocks for worship, we can assemble them in whatever way best facilitates the worship needs for that particular day. These building blocks can be equally used in both the traditional and the contemporary worship styles. Following is a format for a traditional worship service. Notice the key elements in worship that we have highlighted in this chapter.

TRADITIONAL WORSHIP SERVICE
GATHERING AROUND THE WORD

Prelude   *Meditation – Priere*   – Guilmant

During the prelude we encourage you to prepare for worship with silent prayer and meditation. Speak with the Lord. Read the hymns you are about to sing. Meditate on the Scripture of the morning. Expect a special blessing from God today.

Welcome and Sharing of Church Life

(Please sign and pass the *Friendship Book* across the pew.)

Invitation to Worship

Leader: Do not let the wise boast in their wisdom,

People: Do not let the mighty boast in their might,

Leader: Do not let the wealthy boast in their wealth,

All: But let those who boast, boast in this, that they understand and know me, that I am the Lord; I act with steadfast love, justice, and righteousness in the earth, for in these things I delight, says the Lord. (Jeremiah 9:23, 24 NRSV)

Adoration

Hymn No. 131   *Come, Christians, Join to Sing*

Confession

Dear God, we confess that we have sometimes lived like "decaffeinated Christians" – we look like the real thing, but we lack the power! In our pride, we have turned our hearts away from you. We see ourselves pure when we are stained; great when we are small. We have not loved in the way that you love us. We have forgotten to be just and compassionate. We give you thanks for your great love. We praise you for your mercy, which is new every morning. Create in us a desire to live for your glory, rather than for ourselves. Through Christ we pray, Amen.

Thanksgiving

> To God be the glory,
> To God be the glory,
> To God be the glory
> For the things He has done.
> With His blood He has saved me;
> With His power He has raised me;
> To God be the glory for the things He has done.   – Crouch

Supplication

Pastoral Prayer and the Lord's Prayer
(After a prayer request has been spoken, let the people respond,
"Hear our prayers, O Lord.")

PROCLAIMING THE WORD

Scripture Lesson   Matthew 5:1-11

Sermon   *The Way To Go Up Is Down*   Rev. David A. Miller

RESPONDING TO THE WORD

Hymn No. 272 *Just As I Am, Without One Plea* (Verses 1, 3 and 5)

Offering

Offertory by Chancel Choir   *Holy Ground*   – Beatty/Davis
Doxology
Prayer of Thanksgiving

THE SEALING OF THE WORD

Communion

Invitation to the Lord's Table
Words of Institution
Communion Prayer

Distribution of the Bread and Cup
Closing Communion Prayer

BEARING AND FOLLOWING THE WORD INTO THE WORLD

Hymn No. 135   *Fairest Lord Jesus*

Benediction
Postlude   *Overture to "Acina"*   – Handel

This same ACTS pattern of worship is also thoroughly a part of the contemporary worship service format. Below is the program (a better word than "bulletin" for baby boomers) from a contemporary worship service, which follows the same themes presented in the traditional service.

CONTEMPORARY WORSHIP SERVICE

Welcome!
We are so glad you are here this morning. At the beginning of our worship service we pass the red *Friendship Pad* for everyone to sign. We ask everyone to fill in the information on the red pads so that you will know who is worshiping with you today. If you do not have a nametag, you will find them with the red friendship books.

Announcements
During the 9:45 a.m. hour – Children's Sunday School
Sign up for Wonderful Wednesday
Please turn to the Announcement pages for details as well as many other announcements

Praising God in Song
I Will Enter His Gates with Thanksgiving
Almighty
My Life Is In You, Lord
Break through the Chains
The Greatest Thing

Prayer
Drama
Offering
Message   *The Way To Go Up Is Down*   Rev. David A. Miller

Dedication/Praise
   Break through the Chains

Communion
As Communion is being served, we encourage you to hold the bread and cup until all have been served. We will then take the bread and cup in communion with one another. Following communion, we will pass a basket to collect the communion cups.

Communion Songs
   Lord Prepare Me
   There Is Therefore Now No Condemnation

Closing

The contemporary service uses the same basic building blocks of Presbyterian worship but without any labels or particular order. As we analyze each separate part of the service however, the same pattern can be observed.

■ Praising God in Song

I Will Enter His Gates with Thanksgiving: **Entrance** – During this song, the congregation is calling itself to worship. They are reminding themselves of the purpose and goal of worship. There are elements of thanksgiving and adoration as the congregation begins to celebrate God's presence. The words to the music are projected onto a screen, and the people are looking up and singing out. They are clapping their hands, and they have expressions of joy and gladness on their faces. The message is clear – we are entering into God's presence with joy.

Almighty: **Adoration** – As we continue to worship in song, the name of God is exalted and praised.

My Life Is In You: **Thanksgiving** – This song has both elements of **adoration** and **thanksgiving**. At the same time, it is a heartfelt prayer of devotion.

Break through the Chains: **Confession** – The worship leader makes the following comment with synthesized strings playing softly in the background. Notice that this prayer contains many of the same elements as the prayer of **confession** in the traditional service:

> Dear God, we are thankful that even though you are the Almighty Creator of the universe, you are among us this morning. Even though you are fully present, we have not fully opened our lives to you. It's so easy for us to hold back. If we think about it, maybe that is the reason why our lives seem to lack the power that you promise us. This morning, come and break through the chains of our self-centeredness and pride. Meet us now, Lord, as we sing, *Break through the chains.*

The Greatest Thing: The sermon this day is based on the text, "Blessed are the poor in spirit." It will explore the issue of spiritual pride in the Christian life. This song helps to remind the congrega-

tion that Christ and not pride should be on the throne of our lives –
He really is the greatest thing. As we sing this song there are elements
of **adoration** and **dedication** and possibly even **confession**.

■ Prayer

Following the singing, a prayer of **thanksgiving** is offered for the gift
of forgiveness in Christ.

■ Offering

At the conclusion of the offering, a prayer is offered lifting up the
same pastoral concerns that would be shared during the traditional
service..

■ Drama

A drama portrays a conversation between a husband and a wife. In
a humorous way, the drama brings out the fact that the husband and
wife are stuck in the relationship because neither one is willing to let
go of pride and self-centeredness. It becomes clear that the quest for
self-fulfillment does not lead to the instant happiness we often antic-
ipate. As the sermon will later point out, true fulfillment only comes
when we release pride and live with God at the center of our lives.

■ Message

This would be essentially the same as the sermon preached in the traditional worship service. Five percent or less of the message may be
adapted to the younger audience.

■ Dedication/Praise

The service is closed with a prayer, while synthesized strings are playing in the background. During this time there is also a call to **dedication**. Certain prayers are suggested. This section of the service also
contains the element of **confession** in response to the preached
Word. An example of this would be as follows:

> Now this morning we've been talking about pride. Maybe
> you've been so concerned about the faults of others that you

haven't taken the time to really do a spiritual inventory in your own life. Just take a moment now to talk to God about what needs to change. (Music continues to play softly.)

Break through the Chains
We close the service by singing the song *Break through the Chains*. This song becomes a congregational prayer that invites the Holy Spirit to "tear down the strongholds and the walls, and to deliver us from all bondage and strife." Here we are invited to **confession**, **supplication**, and renewed **dedication**.

■ Communion
Just as in the traditional service, the words of institution are proclaimed. In preparation for Communion the congregation sings *Lord Prepare Me*. The communion elements are blessed and distributed among the people. We are reminded as we sing the closing song that *There Is Therefore Now No Condemnation* for those who live in the power of God's grace.

■ Closing
A benediction is said with one or two sentences connecting it to the sermon. The term "closing" is preferred to benediction because the unchurched will more easily understand it.

When we compare these two services, we notice that the instruments, the order of worship, the style of music and the worship language are very different. Yet the essential ingredients necessary for biblical worship are present in each service. From this perspective, these two services are marked more by their common theology of worship than by their stylistic differences. In both service styles we worship Jesus Christ "in spirit and in truth."

Enriching Your Worship

3

When my wife, Leslie, approached her fortieth birthday, I saw a chance to make up for my years of last-minute gifts and underwhelming surprises. I decided to plan a magnificent surprise party. I carefully mapped an intricate strategy full of lavish creativity. When her birthday finally came, Leslie was stunned as a large group of dear friends bellowed the ceremonial "Surprise!" A simpler observance would have communicated to my wife that I loved her, but I wanted a celebration as good as I could make it because she was worth so much to me. Love calls forth a commitment to excellence and beauty.

Sometimes people ask, "Why do you go to all the trouble to fiddle with new technology and plan every detail in the worship service? Can't we worship God by singing a few songs with piano accompaniment?" Yes, but the question misses the point. Authentic love does not demand great expense, but it calls for the very best we can offer. As we offer our sacrifice of praise, are we giving God the best we have to offer? Is our sacrifice "holy and acceptable to God" (Romans 12:1)? Through the birthday party for my wife, I made a special effort to bring joy to her heart. In the Scriptures we find clear descriptions of the kind of worship that delights God. We will find there principles to enrich our worship, no matter what tradition we follow.

Celebration marks the community of Christ. The psalmist writes, "Shout for joy to the Lord, all the earth, burst into jubilant song with music" (Psalms 98:4, NIV). There are more than twenty-five places in the Scripture where we are told to praise God with joyful song. Paul says the grand essentials of the Christian faith are "righteousness and peace and joy in the Holy Spirit" (Romans 14:17). We have reason to celebrate: Christ our Lord is risen and has conquered death for us! Truly we can say, "In your presence there is fullness of joy" (Psalm 16:11). Yes, there is awe in the presence of God. There is also joy, and we know that God delights when we express that joy in public worship. What a shame to plod through the order of worship as though we were performing a checklist of duties or to murmur joyful hymns without emotion. If we learn anything from the psalms of joy, it should be that God wants our worship to express delight. When there is celebration, we tap our toe to the music. Our laughter is spontaneous. We smile. It actually looks like we are enjoying ourselves!

Celebration happens naturally when our focus is on something that brings us joy. At a sporting event, we clap our hands, throw our arms up into the air, and shout so loudly it can make us hoarse. We do not call this emotional; we say we are being supportive of our home team. We are not concerned about what the person next to us might think. Our focus is not on what is happening around us, but what is happening on the playing field. A great enemy of worship is self-consciousness. In our pride we do not want to appear foolish or too emotional. Yet worship is a "beautiful thing" when we worship like Mary, who anointed the feet of Jesus with perfume and then "wiped his feet with her hair" (John 12:3). Authentic worship will yield moments where we sing out for joy. It does not matter if our song is off key or if everything is not just right. Our focus is not on other people; it is on the incredible grace and love of Jesus Christ.

The worship leader with a heart to lead the people into celebration can make effective use of both traditional and contemporary styles. Music is one of the key ways to nurture celebration. Music can create the mood to celebrate.

Joyful songs fire our hearts in worship. They help us feel closer to God. Therefore it is important to integrate into our musical diet upbeat, positive music that stirs our emotions. We should encourage God's people to sing with joy without fear that it will be too emotional. The issue is not drum versus organ. The question is not "Are we high church?" Rather it is "Are we *high worship?*" Does worship lift our spirits so we can experience the joy of the Lord?

The worship service that leads us to celebrate God's goodness should move us toward facing the sin that gnaws at our spirit. We must search our hearts and honestly acknowledge our sin before a Holy God. This is why confession should be a part of our regular pattern of worship. Singing only upbeat songs with a positive, uplifting message can leave worshipers feeling unfulfilled and can frustrate their desire to connect with God in a vital way. Pastor Mark Hiiva describes the necessary link between celebration and confession:

> Contrary to modern fears and philosophies, to join the lament is not a downward spiral into gloom, depression and hopelessness. Nearly every psalm of lament shows us just the opposite. To unburden the heart's troubles to God is the best – indeed, the only – way the heart is freed to hope and celebrate afresh.[1]

As our celebration wakes us to the presence of God, we see our true spiritual need. Paradoxically only then can we truly apprehend God's grace, which leads us back into thanksgiving and joyful praise. As we cry out to God for mercy (Psalm 51:1), he restores to us "the joy of our salvation" (Psalm 51:12). Gerrit Gustafson puts it succinctly, "The fact is, as we approach God's awesome presence, we need a capacity to do both: to leap with unspeakable joy and to weep in prayers of supplication and repentance."[2]

Robert Webber is right: "Worship" is a verb. He notes that one of the legacies of the Reformation is that the people reclaimed the expression of corporate worship. "The Reformers insisted on a form of worship that was distinctly congregational – a worship done by the people."[3]

Passively watching the choir and the ministers worship God is not worship. Robert Wenz goes so far as to quip, "Passive worship is an oxymoron."[4] Worship takes place when we consciously decide to enter into the presence of God.

For some, worship is merely a preliminary to the sermon. "How was church today?" we ask. Many will respond by commenting on the sermon. The alarming reality is that if you were to add up the entire time someone actively sought to worship and respond to the presence of God, it would only amount to a few minutes during the worship service. Today we need to reclaim the Reformation principle that we are a *royal priesthood* and a *kingdom* of priests. Every believer is invited into the most holy place to worship God directly. As priests, we all offer our sacrifices of praise, thanksgiving, and joy (Romans 12:1; Hebrews 13:15).

All of life makes clear that God loves variety. Even identical twins have different fingerprints. It should not surprise us that God loves variety in worship. The psalmist exhorts us to "sing to him a new song, play skillfully, and shout for joy" (Psalm 33:3, NIV). Including variety in our expression of worship should focus upon what will best meet the needs of the people to whom we seek to minister. It is good to treasure the great hymns of our faith, old and new. I have memorized many, and I sing them often. The forms and songs of the historical Church can greatly enrich our worship. So too can contemporary music. Jaroslav Pelikan makes a memorable distinction:

> Tradition is the living faith of the dead; traditionalism is the dead faith of the living. Contemporary worship is a move away from traditionalism. It is not a rejection of the tradition of the living faith. If all we have to celebrate is ourselves and all we have to rely upon is our secular culture, our gatherings

will be "memorial services to a fire gone out."[5]

Tradition is a good servant, but a terrible master. Parts of the worship service that become predictable and automatic tend to become less meaningful and less significant. Just as a faked punt in a football game raises expectations every fourth down for the rest of the game, so even a slight variation in the worship service can rekindle interest and a sense of surprise in worship.

Psalm 150 mentions praising God with at least seven different instruments. This would strongly suggest that every song we sing need not be 300 years old and played only on the organ! Such wide variety hints that no one style of worship is fully adequate. Exhortations to praise God with a certain instrument, or to clap our hands, are *descriptional* rather than *prescriptional*. The point is God seeks to be praised with a variety of traditions and styles.

With so many ways to express the praise of our hearts, we reflect our variety of gifts, styles, temperaments, and life experiences. Bowing our heads or kneeling in prayer can demonstrate a desire to submit to the Lordship of Christ. As we clap our hands, we express our enthusiasm. Lifting our hands can symbolize our surrender to God or our reaching out to embrace him. Throughout the worship service there should be variety in our prayers, our songs, and our sharing of God's word.

Worship should be done "decently and in order" (1 Corinthians 14:40). At the same time, "where the Spirit of the Lord is, there is freedom" (2 Corinthians 3:17). If we are not careful, the order of worship can easily become the worship of order. What is important is to order our services in a way that responds to the call of God for our congregation.

We noted that worship involves communication. We speak to God, and God speaks to us. Let's welcome those spontaneous moments when God moves in our midst! Kennon Callahan writes:

> People don't nod and doze through a service that has integrity and spontaneity. People have a sense of expectancy. Energy

is in the air. People have come anticipating the ways in which God will touch their lives in this service.[6]

On the other hand, there is a danger in overemphasizing freedom. God is not the author of confusion. Unplanned worship can be confusing and disjointed. Good form implies logic, unity, and connectedness throughout the service. Another danger is that the *free tradition* itself can unconsciously evolve into a form more rigid than a historical liturgy. Strive for balance. Plan and prepare to enjoy the spontaneous ways that God may break into our service.

Classic Christian theology teaches that God is both transcendent and immanent. God is present and active in creation. He is near to all who call upon Him in faith. God's immanence lets us intimately know God our Abba Father who tenderly and personally cares for us. God is the lover of our souls who beckons us to "Arise . . . my fair one, and come away with me" (The Song of Solomon 2:10). We feel an intimacy with God when we sing a praise chorus such as "Oh Lord, You're beautiful, Your face is all I see, and when Your eyes are on this child, Your grace abounds to me."[7]

God's immanence speaks of His nearness. God's transcendence speaks of His otherness. God is separate from and above creation. The creator of the universe is worthy to be worshiped. He is the awesome Holy God who sprayed the heavens with stars by merely uttering a word. Our hearts come to know what our eyes cannot perceive, and we are encouraged to realize that God's sovereign power directs our lives. Hymns such as "Holy, Holy, Holy" put us in touch with this dimension of God's character.

In worship it is absolutely vital to keep God's transcendence and God's immanence together, not emphasizing one to the exclusion of the other. Overemphasizing transcendence may mistake God as uncaring and irrelevant, so distant and busy with affairs of the universe that he could not possibly care about us. Overemphasizing immanence misses God's majesty and awe, reducing God to a celestial buddy there only to serve our purposes. Psalm 103 combines the two attributes of God's character:

For as high as the heavens are above the earth *(transcendence)*, so great is his love *(immanence)* for those who fear him. The Lord has established his throne in heaven and his kingdom rules over all *(transcendence)*. As a father has compassion on his children, so the Lord has compassion on those who fear him *(immanence)* (Psalm 103: 11, 19, 13 NIV).

Joy in worship can be contagious. Seekers observe how authentic worship moves believers. With David we could say, "He put a new song in my mouth, a hymn of praise to our God. Many will see and fear and put their trust in the Lord" (Psalm 40:3 NIV).

Paul was sensitive to the outsider's view of worship when he instructed the Corinthian church on how speaking in tongues should be done in an orderly way. He notes the danger of disorder when he writes, "If . . . the whole church comes together and all speak in tongues, and outsiders or unbelievers enter, will they not say that you are out of your mind?" (1 Corinthians 14:23). Paul contrasts this with worship as an effective witness, continuing, "But if all prophesy, an unbeliever or an outsider who enters is reproved by all and called to account by all. After the secrets of the unbeliever's heart are disclosed, that person will bow down before God and worship him, declaring, 'God is really among you'" (1 Corinthians 14:24-25). It is still true today that when seekers come into a church, they can sense the reality of God in the midst of vibrant, Spirit-led worship.

A Lilly Foundation study traced the three crucial factors that led visitors in twenty-six mainline churches across the United States to stay and eventually join those churches. The three answers people gave most were these: The congregation acts like it really believes Jesus is alive. The pastor seems to believe what he or she preaches. The pastor seems to be personable and approachable.[8] Our worship is a witness! It is no accident that the churches that are reaping a harvest among the unchurched are the ones with vibrant and dynamic worship. Our worship does not necessarily help someone understand the content of the Gospel, but it is a great advertisement for the hope and joy that Jesus brings to our lives. Robert Webber sums it up: "Worship is the gospel in motion."[9] Jesus said, "And I, when I am lifted up from the earth, will draw all people to myself" (John 12:32). When we lift up Jesus Christ in heartfelt praise (in spirit) and in a way that is clear to all (in truth), our praise will stir the hearts of seekers and mature Christians.

Some suggest the best way to include seekers in worship is to design a service around seekers' special needs, minimizing aspects of worship that could be offensive or unappealing to them. [This approach assumes the primary purpose of coming together is evangelism, not worship. Willow Creek Community Church, which has had phenomenal success reaching the unchurched, goes so far as to say that worship is something "seekers cannot understand or appreciate" and "worship and seekers do not mix."[10] In the special services, most of the music is performed by artists, prayers are brief, confession is rarely emphasized, and the sermon is designed to speak to the unbeliever or new Christian. The message is positive and practical. Such a service may serve as an evangelistic rally, but it leaves out an essential aspect of worship, the desire to encounter the living God in spirit and in truth.]

Sally Morgenthaler argues persuasively that seeker-driven services actually lose a significant number of unchurched people because the services dilute true biblical worship and underestimate the positive impact God-centered worship can have. She writes:

> The most significant benefit of a worship service is connecting with God. It doesn't matter how chatty and interesting the celebrity interviews, how captivating the drama, how stunning the soloist, or how relevant the message. When personal interaction with God is absent, the church loses much of its appeal.[11]

[Our goal is to be sensitive to the needs of the seekers by communicating clearly, by treating them with respect, and by allowing them to respond in a way that is truly heartfelt. It is possible to relate the service to the needs of the seeker without leaving out important aspects of Christian worship.]

In *Room for God?* Robert Wenz warns against what he sees as human-centered tendencies in the church growth/contemporary worship movement.[12] He notes that Paul encouraged the church at Corinth to be seeker sensitive and not to repel unbelievers with chaotic and unintelligible worship. Wenz goes on to say:

> There is no suggestion from God's Word that prophets should proclaim a more sensitive message, a message that humans have merely not lived up to their potential – a message that avoids making unbelievers feel "convicted by all" that they are sinners. Nor is there instruction to preach only the inclusive message of God's love so that unbelievers will be able to stand tall before God by faith rather than fall down before him and say, "God is really among you."

Wenz's caution is a good counterbalance. Worship should be designed to be understood, not just to be inoffensive.

[While Wenz is helpful in pointing out the potential dangers of focusing on the needs of the worshiper, he creates a false polarity between our satisfaction and God's glorification.] Jesus said, "Let anyone who is thirsty come to me." (John 7:37). Notice he does not say, "All who are thirsty should repent of their self-centered need for water. They are coming to me to meet their own need, rather than to glorify me." Instead, Jesus encourages the thirsty to come looking for the Living Water. Our problem is not that we are coming and asking for living water, but that we are seeking in the wrong place. As Jeremiah pointed out long ago, we are drinking from "broken and polluted cisterns" (Jeremiah 2:13) rather than the Living Water of Christ (John 4:13). We are trying to exist on a few scraps of bread, rather than feeding on the living manna that comes down from heaven (John 6:33-35). Throughout the Gospels, Jesus invites us to respond to God's command, not on the basis of duty, but on the basis of rewards. Jesus constantly appeals to our self-interest with such statements as "Do not store up for yourselves treasures on earth

. . . but store up for yourselves treasures in heaven" (Matthew 6:19, 20). Denying self does not mean that we deny our self-interest. Rather it means that we deny a distorted self-image that has been warped by pride.

In the Incarnation the transcendent, eternal Word is made flesh and accessible to the language, culture, and heart-song of the people. Worship should also be accessible and in the language of the people. Entering a church should not feel like entering a subculture 200 years removed from our own. In contrast, contemporary music and words communicate a subliminal relevance, not to candles burning softly in a dark sanctuary, but relevance to the everyday world of working, loving, eating, and playing. Worship connects to the real hurts and hopes of life. Foreign music and language will have a subliminal irrelevance. We will associate the music with something other-worldly and only for Sunday.

Even if a church makes the decision not to have a contemporary worship service, it is still important to integrate contemporary elements congruent with its style of worship. The language of Scripture included the everyday phrases of its first Hebrew and Greek readers. Likewise the language we use in church today should be the usage familiar to the modern ear. Contemporary instruments may accompany or sometimes replace the organ or piano. Contemporary praise choruses arranged in classical settings can enrich the music.

Questions for Discussion

1. Does your worship service feel more like a festival or a funeral?
2. Do you agree that God wants us to demonstrate our joy in worship? If so, why?
3. Describe the times when you feel most like you are participating in worship.
4. Do you think we have enough variety in congregational worship? Why or why not?
5. Are there any archaic aspects to our worship?
6. Agree or disagree:

   -In our services we do well at nurturing a sense of awe in worship.

   -In our denomination we struggle to demonstrate joy in worship.

   -Most of us are geared toward presentation rather than participation.

Designing Your Contemporary Worship Service

We live in an era of the thirty-second sound byte. Good communication touches the five senses. Visual images predominate. All across America, churches have reordered their worship services to accommodate this new communication style. This new service is often called *a contemporary worship service*. The following components are usually present in such a service:

Music in a "light rock" style or other styles such as country and western, reggae, rhythm and blues, rap, jazz, and alternative rock.

Use of a band – key instruments include drums, guitar, bass, and synthesizer. Flute, saxophone, trumpet, violin, tambourine, and conga drums may be included.

Music led by a small group of vocalists, often called a *praise team*, who sing along with the congregation.

Projecting the words to the music onto a screen.

Several songs sung back to back with the music blending the

songs together.

Message given from the center of chancel, rather than from behind a pulpit.

Personal testimony usually related to the theme of the service.

Drama to illustrate a key point in the sermon.

Occasional use of liturgical dance.

Choice of an informal venue, perhaps in buildings that reflect contemporary architecture.

Informal, interactive communication.

Freedom to clap and be demonstrative in worship.

An abundance of plants and flowers in the sanctuary.

Little or no liturgy (traditional creeds, prayers of confession, doxologies, and Gloria Patris appear less frequently); no bulletins or robes.

Herb Miller adds the following characteristics:

High congregational participation early in the service.

A much greater emphasis on beginning with enthusiasm and energy, rather than beginning with solemnity and quiet meditation.

An overall feeling of liveliness and creativity, rather than solemn sameness.

Adjustments in lighting for mood, transitions, etc.

Casual attire.

Point made in the sermons to sound less academic and more practical – the preacher often avoids *churchy* language in service.[1]

Charles Trueheart gives this general description of contemporary worship: "No crosses, no robes, no clerical collars . . . no biblical gobbledygook, no prayerly rote . . . no pipe organs, no dreary Eighteenth-Century hymns, no forced solemnity, no Sunday finery."[2]

Why Start a Contemporary Worship Service?

Is a contemporary worship service right for your church? The primary reason for starting a contemporary worship service is to broaden the outreach of your church. Think of the new service as a gift to those in your community whom you are not currently reaching. Let the agenda of the new service be shaped by the needs of these unchurched people rather than by other priorities of the church.

Starting a contemporary service provides the opportunity to deploy new talent in your church. Elements like a band, a praise team, and a drama team may in a significant way involve people who had little involvement in the traditional service. Their families and friends may become actively involved. One church that started a contemporary worship service began a Sunday school class for erstwhile musicians and their friends. After a jam session, they conduct a brief Bible study and share prayer concerns. Once a month they play in the service. Such a class would make little sense if there were no place for popular music in the ministry of the church.

A contemporary worship service will have a positive effect on the Sunday morning church attendance. This is really more a happy by-product than a reason for such a service, but the fact is the greater the choices, the greater the participation. Our focus in starting such services should be to grow in mission, not merely to grow in numbers. True growth in the congregation will only take place when we serve the needs in our community, rather than maintaining the institution of the church.

A contemporary service will nurture celebration in worship.

Celebration is possible both in the traditional and contemporary styles, but in the contemporary style the tempo creates a feeling of *rock*, which adds to the exuberance in worship. In a survey of nineteen Presbyterian Church (USA) congregations that added a contemporary worship service, respondents described the benefits of the service to the church. Many spoke of the energy and enthusiasm for worship generated during the worship. They spoke of "a great sense of freedom and power in worship – a vital sense of energy, joy, and love," and "more joyful celebration." All these churches had existing traditional worship, yet it is clear they discovered a new level of celebration in worship.

A contemporary service offers additional resources for worship. Worship flows smoothly if there can be a mixing of songs that involve celebration, exaltation, and reflection. Praise choruses mixed with the great hymns of the faith can greatly facilitate an extended time of worship. Many passages in the Psalms have been set to contemporary music. The length and the style of contemporary choruses blend beautifully with many passages in the Psalms. For example, Psalm 100 would be too short for most hymns, but set to contemporary music, it becomes an excellent song to sing as the congregation gathers for worship. Singing these psalms together allows us to live out the biblical command to "sing psalms, hymns, and spiritual songs to God" (Colossians 3:16).

If you decide to start a contemporary worship service, what type of contemporary worship service do you want it to be? The service will embody the vision for ministry of your church. Churches that emphasize evangelism may want to design a service that is seeker-driven. A church that follows a more liturgical tradition may incorporate communion every Sunday, and churches that highly value pastoral care and community service may allow specific time for the sharing of needs. Rather than re-creating a service used by another church, your service should meet the needs of your people in a way that is congruent with your church's priorities and established traditions.

There is no *right* approach. We have already noted that music is a "disputable matter." The right path for your church is the one that makes for the greatest peace, unity, and effective mission. Sometimes a congregation will live happily with two different styles of worship. Others will seek to integrate contemporary worship into a traditional service. Many will go through a process of trying several different approaches to integrating contemporary worship until they discover what works best. (For a case study of a church that went through this kind of process, see Case Study V, Glendale Presbyterian Church.) To discover what is right for your church, examine the three basic models for contemporary worship.

In the *blended contemporary worship service*, traditional and contemporary styles are employed in a significant way. Such services go from "Bach to rock" all on the same morning. If the church previously employed a traditional style, traditional elements usually predominate in such blended services. A newly planted church may want to emphasize the contemporary style of worship.[3]

If there is at least a 60/40 blend in the two styles, the service truly will be blended. An occasional new tune played on the organ, giving it a decidedly traditional feel, does not constitute a blended service. One of the acid tests is the presence of a set of drums in the sanctuary. The contemporary style is truly present when a full-scale band is allowed to play during the service.

A blended approach offers the following advantages:

- Each service reinforces the philosophy that both styles are legitimate and have a place in worship.

- Greater unity in the membership is possible if you have two blended services on Sunday morning – members don't have to choose one style versus another.

- A smaller church can use limited resources effectively. (For a case study of a small church that went from traditional to blended, with many positive results, see Case Study VII,

Buechel Presbyterian Church.)

- Combining hymns that emphasize the cognitive with praise choruses that emphasize the emotive, broadens the experience of worship.

- We remember the needs of others in worship.

A blended contemporary worship service has the greatest possibility of success when the following factors are in place:

The church began with a blended style of worship.

The pastor has a clear and well-articulated vision for blended worship.

The lay leadership and the staff embrace and support this vision.

The church is open to innovation and change.

The church places a very high priority on missions and evangelism.

The pastor introduces change in a steady, patient, and sensitive way.

Be encouraged by the pastor who wanted to move the church piano from one side of the chancel to the other. Knowing that this would be controversial, the pastor decided to move the piano exactly one inch every week. By the time the piano had reached the other side, not only was it unnoticed but also most people couldn't remember the piano being anywhere else! With the blended approach this is the pace of change needed to avoid destructive controversy.

The benefits of blended worship are significant, but if three or more of these factors are weak, a blended style of worship may cause major controversy. This can happen when there is just enough of each style to offend everyone!

Jesus knew even Spirit-led change does not come easily. He said, "No one puts new wine into old wineskins; otherwise the wine will burst the skins, and the wine is lost, and so are the skins; but one puts new wine into fresh wineskins" (Mark 2:22). There are two important lessons in this parable. First, whenever God brings renewal into the life of His church, it creates new structure. Throughout the history of the church, new music has been an element of renewal. As the church goes beyond itself to reap a harvest among the lost, it inevitably begins to sing a new song. As the artificial barriers of language and style disappear, believing hearts receive the message of Christ. The growth of contemporary music is a sign of the renewal that God is bringing in our day. As always, the old wineskins are not ready to receive the new wine.

The second point Jesus makes is that if you try to combine the "new wine in the old wineskins," it will cause the "old wineskins to be ruined." When a church is more focused on the forms of worship than on the essentials, it will almost certainly reject this new wine. Indeed it can ruin the peace and unity of a church.

The solution Jesus offers is "to pour new wine into new wineskins." New expressions in worship may require new structures for worship. This leads us to the second type of contemporary worship service, which I call an *alternative/contemporary worship service*. That is a weekly contemporary worship service as an alternative worship experience to traditional worship. The approach may actually take a variety of forms. Charles Trueheart describes an Episcopal church in Orange County, California, that offered a traditional, a contemporary, and a charismatic service on Sunday morning. Solona Beach (California) Presbyterian Church takes a similar approach. They offer contemporary, blended, and "high church" traditional services. Our discussion here will deal with adding only a second style of worship, but the principles relate to adding multiple styles.

A second service is usually styled to appeal to churched or

unchurched baby boomers and busters. If there are not many of these age groups in the church, the service is started for people who are not there yet! Most of the components of contemporary worship we noted earlier are present in this service. An *alternative/contemporary* service is distinguished from the blended in that it will rarely use the sound of a pipe organ. Robes will probably seem out of place. Casual communication replaces formal liturgy. The music is predominantly contemporary. An *alternative/contemporary* service may use parts of Christian liturgy, but written calls to worship, creeds, The Lord's Prayer, and responsive readings will probably appear less frequently. To broaden communication, drama and video clips will be introduced freely throughout the service.

There is evidence to indicate that including traditional elements of worship in the contemporary service actually has a very positive effect with the unchurched. One recent study indicated that 47 percent of the unchurched said they would like to come back to a church service where they could sing some traditional hymns.[4] Another study found that 65 percent of Americans prefer churches that provide a mix of traditional and contemporary music.[5]

The *alternative/contemporary* model provides some very strong advantages, and when you offer it along with a traditional service you can double your outreach. Someone in your church may have a young family with kids living next door. Two houses down, there is an older couple who have been lifelong Presbyterians. The younger couple may be more inclined to the contemporary service. The lifelong Presbyterians may prefer the traditional style. An enthusiastic invitation could be given to each neighbor.

Abruptly changing the structure of a service that has existed for years is a surefire way to start a major uproar within a church. Giving choices tends to diminish tension. The same person who objects strenuously to contemporary praise choruses in the traditional service may be neutral or even positive about *the young people singing their songs* in another service.

An *alternative/contemporary* service allows different parts of the

church to worship in their heart-song. In a blended service, each part
of the congregation must endure another's style of worship that is not
in their heart-song. As a result members may drift off to other
churches that offer the style of worship they desire. The Chinese
United Methodist Church of Los Angeles faced a comparable
dilemma:

> The church was primarily ministering to Chinese-born immi-
> grants, and they were losing their English-speaking,
> American-born children from the church. Their primary wor-
> ship service was given in both Cantonese and English. After
> preaching in Cantonese, the pastor would switch to English
> and give the same message. While he was speaking in
> Cantonese, the English-speakers would quickly write notes or
> read their Bibles. When he spoke in English, the Cantonese
> speakers would do the same. The end result was that no one
> was happy, the service was long, and the English-speaking
> youth were leaving.[6]

Happily the Chinese church was able to solve its problem by
starting two new services.

An *alternative/contemporary* service can be introduced quickly,
while it may take years to blend contemporary elements into traditional worship. An *alternative/contemporary* worship service, however,
has the potential to create conflict and disunity. Will two different
styles of worship feel like two different churches? Marva Dawn thinks
the alternative/contemporary approach will cause more harm than
good. She argues:

> Throughout the country I've seen how divisive that can
> become. Moreover the split between traditional and contem-
> porary usually divides a parish along age lines, and conse-
> quently, younger and newer believers lose the opportunity to
> gain from the faith experience of older members.[7]

While a division along age lines is possible, it is not inevitable. At least 30 percent of baby boomers may prefer traditional worship.[8] Some people in the builder generation will be drawn by the exuberance and the informality of the contemporary service. Dawn's position assumes that there is an even mix of ages in the traditional, mainline church, yet seniors far outnumber the young in most churches. An alternative/contemporary approach may bring more of a balance to the age demographic. As people meet in common forums such as Sunday school or midweek programs, they have a greater opportunity to get to know one another and build mutual respect.

Dawn also reports the complaint that changing the familiar service indicates "a greater concern for 'people out there' than for people in the pew—an attitude that demonstrates an inadequate understanding of what worship is for."[9] But keep in mind that worship is for God. It is God who tells us that he delights when he is praised in many languages. To insist that everyone speak "my language for worship" can lead to pride and ethnocentrism. Are we willing to broaden our cultural style so that "the people out there" can relate fully to the worship?

Dawn's next objection is, "Such a split allows a congregation to escape talking about worship . . . about the weaknesses and strengths of various styles."[10] Yet perhaps it can lead to fruitful discussion. Is style really what unifies us? What are the biblical essentials for worship? Churches need to talk more, not less, about the essential ingredients of worship. Having separated style from substance, we can understand the weaknesses and strengths of the various styles.

In addition to Dawn's concerns, I would add a fourth potential drawback to the *alternative/contemporary* worship service approach. Spiritual pride may lead one group to assert that their worship is more spiritual and pleasing to God. If the contemporary worship service grows larger than the traditional service, the supporters of the traditional service may feel threatened and defensive. If the pastor is too closely identified with one service, it may communicate an inappropriate preference.

These very real problems are potentially traumatic in the life of a congregation, but these steps of preparation and consensus building can foster a sense of unity amidst the diversity.

- Preach on themes that will build unity and peace and nurture a sense of family within the church. Preach the same sermon at all services.

- Emphasize the outreach dimension of the contemporary worship service. Describe it as "a gift to the community." As often as possible, connect it to the part of your mission statement that refers to the church's outreach.

- Listen to the needs of the community, the needs of the congregation, and the collective wisdom of the key leadership of the church. Work at developing unity among the leadership. Staff trips to conferences or a one-day seminar at the church can help the leadership catch a common vision for worship. Be sensitive and inclusive of the worshiping needs of the entire congregation whenever worship is addressed.

- If possible, schedule a common Sunday school hour where the two congregations can interact. Create a common fellowship hour every Sunday morning where people from each service can meet each other. Encourage your congregation to elect church officers from each of the services. Print the order of worship for both services in one common bulletin. This will help the membership to be aware of what is happening at the service they do not attend, and a visitor is more likely to notice the options available for worship. Program activities that will bring people from the different services together. First Presbyterian Church in Yakima, Washington, started a once-a-month "prayer and praise fest." This service offers blended worship around the theme of healing.

• During the first year, schedule at least two congregational forums to allow people to raise concerns and questions. Create several feedback loops to improve communication. Congregational forums can be a healthy way for the congregation to dialogue about changes in worship. Scheduling elders to be available following the worship service to talk with anyone who has concerns gives people a chance to talk one on one about their differences. Discourage *we/they* language when referring to the various services.

Church for the Unchurched

Some communities call out for a special service for persons with no experience with the Christian Church. It may be called a seeker service or a proclamation event. These services proclaim faith in Jesus Christ using familiar elements – video clips, secular songs, drama, and dance – to share the message of salvation. What makes this service different from an evangelistic event is that it is offered weekly.

The seeker service will only be successful if the Christians in the church are committed to inviting their non-Christian friends to such a service on a regular basis. Grace Community Fellowship in Baltimore, Maryland, offers both a "seeker sensitive" contemporary worship service and a "seeker targeted" contemporary service on the same Sunday. Both events are growing and making an impact on the congregation. "Eighty-nine percent of the people who had been at Grace for a year or more had invited an unchurched person to a corporate function."[11] The seeker service must be held in a building other than the sanctuary to help break down barriers with the unchurched. A good public address system, a quality band, and video projection become more essential in this service. As Paul went into the marketplace to engage the Greeks in discussion about God, so today's Christians meet unbelievers on their own familiar ground to tell them about Jesus Christ. The preaching of George Whitefield, John Wesley, D. L. Moody, and Billy Graham follows the example of the early church in taking the Gospel to the unchurched.

Congregational singing is de-emphasized in favor of a live performance by the band. After all, the new congregation may begin as spec-
tators. Because of the performance aspect of this service, there is a
need for a great deal of planning and rehearsal.

There are several reasons for starting this type of service:

> This approach makes evangelism a central priority of the
> church. A sad truth today is that many churches talk about
> evangelism, but in practice it rarely happens. One study sug-
> gests that the average church introduces only 1.7 people to
> Christ per year for every hundred people attending worship.[12]
> A *Christianity Today* study reported that "only one percent of
> its readership had recently shared the Gospel."[13]

> The seeker service allows church members to do the work of
> evangelism at a time when the unchurched are most likely to
> attend. Even though many in our culture view Sunday not as
> a holy day but as a holiday, Sunday morning still provides a
> very strategic opportunity to invite a friend to come to the
> church's "seeker service." This event forces members to take
> seriously the challenge to invite friends. The whole event is
> geared toward reaching seekers. If few seekers are present, the
> event may no longer be offered.

> The seeker service allows the church to target a group within
> its community not being reached by the Gospel, for example
> to reach out to Generation X. Often this service is offered on
> a Saturday night.

Before you start a seeker service, consider the following problems
associated with such a service.

> The amount of time and effort demanded of staff and volun-
> teers to maintain a seeker service is very costly.

A seeker service is not truly a worship experience.[14] Since the goal is really evangelism and not worship, often the service leaves out key ingredients, such as confession and petition. Some churches have understood this and offer a "believer service" either at another hour on Sunday morning or sometime during the week (usually Wednesday night). In effect this makes many of those who embrace the seeker service "Third-Day Adventists" since they are departing from the biblical pattern of worshiping on the Lord's Day. Of even greater significance is that this model underestimates the positive impact vibrant worship can have on the unchurched. For the churches that do not have a true worship alternative, a seeker service is an inadequate substitute for worship.

There are indeed many tensions and potential problems that come with starting a contemporary worship service. No matter what kind you start, the bottom line is that it is worth the effort! It is better to be in a church where there are tensions and struggles around the issue of outreach in worship than a church that has harmony and peace but no real sense of mission.

Questions for Discussion

1. Do you want your contemporary worship service to be a gift to the community?

2. Which of the types of contemporary worship services appeal most to you? Which do you think would fit your church the best?

3. Agree or Disagree? The contemporary worship service alongside a traditional worship service on Sunday morning does not necessarily lead to division and conflict within a church.

4. In what ways can you make any change in worship feel like something added rather than something taken away?

Starting a Contemporary Service: A Twenty-Point Checklist

5

Once you decide to explore the possibility of initiating a new contemporary worship service, there are practical points to consider. Here in brief are important steps to take.

1. *Develop a thriving traditional service.*

As long as the traditional service is growing and alive, addition of another style of service will not feel like a threat to the unity of your church. The sanctuary will not feel uncomfortably empty when some members attend the new alternative. As you launch the contemporary service, consider ways to enrich existing services. Choir cantatas, theme Sundays featuring expert speakers, or other special events may reassure those who prefer the traditional style that their service is valued in the life of the church.

2. *Lay a strong foundation with your church leaders.*

There must be a common vision for worship. If you know where you are headed, you can avoid confusion and frustration every time a decision needs to be made. First and foremost, gather with your leadership and pray that the Holy Spirit will guide you to the model for worship that is best for the church. Study and discuss the issue of worship and how your church's public worship relates to evangelism and service to your community. Sponsor forums where a cross section of the church can talk, and seek opportunities for key staff and elders to attend workshops related to contemporary worship. Sunday school provides an appropriate venue for education on these issues. A series of sermons on worship can communicate the theological basis for offering a new style of worship experience in your church.

3. Identify your existing congregation and describe your target audience.

The most strategic part of planning is to identify your congregation and the people they desire to serve. Charles Arn offers the following chart as a way of identifying a target audience.[1] Begin by classifying the largest number of people in the congregation; for example, in Chart 1, we see that seniors are the majority in this studied church. Next, identify your target audience, the part of your community you want to reach. This church has decided to start a service for boomers (persons ages 33-51) who are seekers. They could further ask if they want their seeker service to be seeker-driven or seeker-sensitive. In Chart 1, the church has decided to start a seeker-driven service.

Chart 1

Target Audience	CONGREGATION		
	19-32 Busters	33-51 Boomers	52+ Seniors
Christians			(seniors)
Seekers — Sensitive / Driven		(boomers, driven)	

Chart 2 represents a church that decided to start a seeker-sensitive service that will reach out to boomers who are Christians as well as to seekers.

Chart 2

CONGREGATION			
Target Audience	**19-32** **Busters**	**33-51** **Boomers**	**52+** **Seniors**
Christians			
Sensitive Seekers Driven			

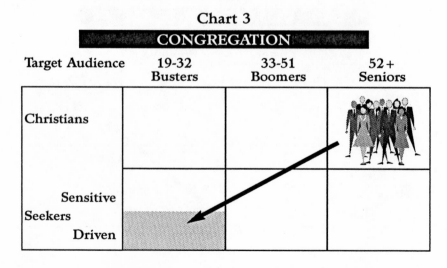

The further the target group is from your largest group, the more obstacles there will be to overcome. For example, in Chart 3 a congregation with a majority of seniors has decided to reach out to non-Christian baby busters. Such a strategy may well be the leading of the Holy Spirit, but there will be many obstacles to overcome. (For a case study of how these obstacles can be overcome, see Case Study VIII, Brunswick Prebyterian Church.)

Chart 3

CONGREGATION			
Target Audience	**19-32** **Busters**	**33-51** **Boomers**	**52+** **Seniors**
Christians			
Sensitive Seekers Driven			

Chart 4 represents a church that has decided to move in one direction, but into two groups – boomers and busters. This strategy is viable because there is significant common ground between the boomer and buster generation.

Chart 4

	CONGREGATION		
Target Audience	19-32 Busters	33-51 Boomers	52+ Seniors
Christians	←	←	
Sensitive Seekers Driven			

Chart 5 represents a church that has decided to reach out in two opposite directions. Since there may be little that appeals to both groups, a good strategy would be to start two completely different services.

Chart 5

	CONGREGATION		
Target Audience	19-32 Busters	33-51 Boomers	52+ Seniors
Christians	←		→
Sensitive Seekers Driven			

God will be honored when your church reaches out to embrace any portion of the population as long as your intention is to include, not exclude.

4. Recruit a contemporary worship service planning team.

No one can do everything! Beginning a new program of any sort in the church demands attention to many details. Participants in an active worship committee can do such things as scheduling, assessing needs for space and equipment, reviewing budget, planning how to conduct the service, organizing drama and banner ministries, and returning valuable feedback to the pastor.

The lead time necessary to begin the service will vary depending on the staff and resources available. Seven to nine months is probably ample time for thorough planning.

5. Agree on a mission statement for the new service.

Communicating clearly the purpose of the new endeavor will express the unity and commitment of your church. A process similar to identifying the target audience will clarify direction and increase enthusiasm for a shared goal. Is the service for evangelism or will it provide an alternative style for current young members? Is the purpose to attract new people or to relieve overcrowding in existing facilities? Will the new service blend old *and* new styles or create an opportunity to worship in traditional *or* contemporary fashion at different times or places?

Having clarified the purpose, it is time to ask what to call the service. The label we put on the service will impact its success. Churches around the country have chosen a variety of titles: The Band Service, a functional title associating "band" with contemporary music; Connections, emphasizing the effort to help the church connect with a broad range of individuals; Celebration Service, to focus on joy and celebration, a name attractive both to the seeker and the committed Christian. Other labels I've seen are Intersections, Informal Worship, or even a neutral 9:45 a.m. Service, or fourth service, or the Saturday Night Service.

Contemporary Worship is the name chosen most often.[2] This communicates cultural relevance and is used in a positive way within our culture. On the other hand, "contemporary" is hard to define, and for builders and seniors, it represents ideas which are highly threatening.

6. Plan your funding.

The cost of starting a new service will vary depending on the compatibility and availability of a location for the service, audiovisual and technical resources, and allocation of staff. Both large and small churches can enjoy success, however; for a description of a smaller church that found creative ways to finance their new service see Case Study IV, New Covenant Presbyterian Church.)

Budget considerations may seem like a very elementary step, but it is possible to get so excited about the thought of a new service that we fail to plan for needed funds. Needs for the first year might include salaries for contemporary worship leader and musicians/band; paper, printing, and copyright licensing fees for music or drama sketches; sound system and projection equipment; banners or other accessories; and costs for direct mail or advertising the service to the community.

Even when the projected cost is great, remember that the new service will draw in new people who help pay for these costs. Seven dollars a week from 25 households will supply $9,100. If participation doubles in two years, $18,200 will have the service well on its way to being self-supporting.

7. Share with your leadership various models for contemporary worship.

It's a good idea to visit churches in the area that have thriving contemporary worship services. This will help clarify your target audience and purpose. Continue making such visits during the first year of your service.

8. Have your congregation participate in a contemporary worship service.

Even a small amount of exposure to the contemporary style will help your congregation prepare for changes that will come in the future. After the leadership has had a chance to study the issues and talk about what kind of service might be best, plan a contemporary worship service in place of the regular traditional service. Let your congregation know that on this Sunday you want them to see and experience what is being planned for another hour.

You may choose to tone it down, but make sure the introductory event allows the congregation as a whole to understand the flavor and mood of the new service. The sermon could focus on a theme that would build a common vision for worship. In my church, we called this Sunday "Celebration Sunday." Afterward we did an informal survey among our membership to learn how they felt about the dynamics of this service.

9. Recruit the worship leader.

The worship leader will be a major factor in defining and shaping the contemporary worship service. Worship is essentially pastoral in nature because in worship we experience God's healing, sustaining, and guiding presence. Worship reconciles us to God and to one another in new and sometimes profound ways. When choosing the worship leader, the pastor is delegating a very important part of ministry. It isn't enough only to be able to sing and play a musical instrument! The worship leader should possess a commitment to nurture spiritual growth and a belief that worship is the central priority of Christian life and that all worship should be done in a sincere and heartfelt way. The leader should demonstrate the spiritual maturity to offer encouraging words, meaningful prayers, and challenging insights during worship. A commitment to work in a congenial and mutually supportive relationship with a pastor, musicians, and staff will be essential to unity and success.

10. Build a praise team, praise band, drama team, and sound team.

The praise team consists of the singers who lead the congregation during the singing. They do not sing *to* the congregation, but *with* the congregation. Their role is to facilitate worship through music.

The drama team will greatly enhance the communication process. The joy and devotion they display is as important as artistic talent! They should establish rapport with the target audience you want to reach.

Music is the key ingredient that makes a contemporary worship service dynamic and attractive, and key to the music is the quality of the band and sound mix. If the church does not have someone who is highly skilled in sound engineering, it would be wise to spend the money necessary to hire an outside consultant.

Sometimes a church will settle for anyone who will volunteer for these roles, but it is important to begin with people who can produce a service others will find appealing. It is relatively easy to recruit someone to a position of leadership, but asking them to step down can create hard feelings that can linger for years. If you have musicians who want to play but do not fit in with the vision for the service, try to find a way to involve them occasionally for special music in the service.

11. Aim for excellence.

You do not have to have the ideal before you begin. Use the best talent and equipment you can afford. Incorporate the skills and gifts of members of your congregation who can dance, lead worship, play instruments, or skillfully operate audiovisual equipment in ways that glorify God.

12. Plan to use synthesized sound.

MIDI computer technology gives even a church with limited resources exciting options for improving the quality of the music. A MIDI computer and/or MIDI keyboard are the major pieces of equipment necessary to provide the synthesized sound. If the church has a key-weighted synthesizer, anyone who can play the piano can be trained to play the MIDI. This technology is versatile and offers obvious advantages over prerecorded music.

13. Try to add to, rather than take away from, the current worship schedule.

Change is easier when people are assured that what they greatly value will not be discarded. After all, our goal is not to change artistic preferences, but to share God's word with all people in ways that are meaningful. For a community of newcomers who speak another language, the church might consider adding a service they can understand. In the same way, consider adding a worship service for people in a different age or cultural community who find meaning in other styles of expression.

14. Begin at an hour that is friendly to your target audience.

Sunday morning is often the best. Fewer activities compete for the time and attention of the unchurched at this hour. Research indicates no more than 20 percent of Saturday evening services survive more than a year.[3] Survey and discuss the schedule that promises best attendance in your area. Whether your target audience prefers a weekday, Saturday, or Sunday, remember your mission. The best techniques and most expensive equipment will be wasted if the worship service does not meet the people at their point of need. (For a case study of a church that added a Saturday evening service that has been well attended, see Case Study VI, Menlo Park Presbyterian Church.)

15. Identify elements that build unity.

Chapter 4 noted important steps to build unity amidst diversity of worship style. A divisive and disgruntled congregation will not embody the principles you want to model for seekers and new members.

16. Start at a strategic time of the year.

An ideal time to start a contemporary worship service would be on a high attendance Sunday, such as Easter when many churches normally have an additional service to accommodate the larger numbers. By starting the service when people are more likely to come, you will create a very positive first impression with those you are seeking to reach.

If you are changing a previously existing Sunday morning worship schedule, birth the service at a natural time for transition. For example, if your church changes from a summer schedule to a school-year schedule in early fall, this might be the ideal time to start a new contemporary worship service.

17. Start strong and stay strong.

Work to achieve "critical mass" within the first six months. Ideally your service will attract enough people to make the sanctuary feel comfortably full, perhaps at 50 percent of the seating capacity of the sanctuary. When launching a rocket, 80 percent of the fuel is spent in getting the rocket off the launch pad. This is a critical phase of the flight. The critical phase of the contemporary worship service will be the first six months. If people perceive it as a dynamic and growing service, growth will naturally follow. On the other hand, if the sanctuary is uncomfortably empty and the singing is weak, the contemporary worship service may look like a failure.

In one church I served, we built up the attendance during the first month through a special challenge. The Sunday before our first service, I challenged the congregation to consider attending both old and new services for a month. About sixty people responded to the challenge. These sixty greatly helped us to quickly achieve critical mass. Later many of these people returned to the traditional service. Fortunately their seats were quickly taken by newcomers. The contemporary service was off and growing.

18. Use advertising.

Given the critical nature of the launch phase of your service, it would be wise to invest in advertising. Perhaps a local newspaper will run a story on your new service. When we began our service, I approached the editor of a large newspaper from the angle that contemporary worship was a national trend beginning to redefine the look of American churches. She felt this was a story worth covering, and the paper printed a major article on this theme and devoted several paragraphs to our initiative.

19. Develop a follow-up plan for visitors.

As you commit to a contemporary worship service, ask, "What are we going to do if it works?" Leaders might write personalized follow-up cards to all who visit in the first three months. Have your follow-up plan ready to put into effect as soon as your service begins. The best advertising campaign will mean little if there is no effective follow-up.

20. Conduct a thorough public relations campaign with your congregation.

The time to begin to talk about the emerging contemporary worship service is long before it ever comes into existence. If you are studying the possibility of a contemporary worship service with your leadership, publicize the effort with your congregation. Invite their comments and encourage them to pray with you and for you. Once the leadership has decided to start a service, keep the congregation fully abreast at every step. Help them understand the reason for the service. Describe in detail what the service will look like. You know you have done your job well when the congregation is on tiptoes to see who is going to come and what God is going to do the day you launch your first service.

Questions for Discussion

1. Does this planning process make you feel as if a contemporary service is within reach, or does it make you feel completely overwhelmed?

2. As you think through this planning process, which steps will be more easily accomplished? Where will you encounter the greatest difficulty?

3. Who do you think should be the target audience for your church?

4. What would be the best way for you to expose your wider congregation to the various elements of a contemporary worship service?

5. What would be the best time of year for your church to start such a service?

Case Studies

─────────────────────────────────────── 6

Introduction to the Case Studies

Is contemporary worship just a fad? Will it lose its attractiveness after the novelty wears off? What will our service look like five years from now? What changes will we go through over a ten-year period?

The following case studies of Presbyterian churches around the country strengthen the point that contemporary worship is here to stay. These churches happen to be Presbyterian, but the issues and challenges they face are universal. Taken together these case studies provide a practical look at the kinds of conflicts, programs, costs, and planning that go into starting and maintaining a contemporary worship service. They also show the impact contemporary worship can have in the life and ministry of the congregation.

I chose these churches to show how contemporary worship works in a variety of congregations. They range in size from small to very large and geographically from coast to coast. I highlighted the most significant contributions of each church in the "Key Learning Points" section of each case study. The first four churches (Church at the Center, Grand Haven, Mt. Holly, and New Covenant) feature alternative contemporary services. The next three churches (Glendale,

Menlo Park, and Buechel) demonstrate the blended worship approach. The final church (Brunswick) could be characterized as a seeker service.

Adding a new service was not easy in any of the churches studied, but the benefits have proven to be significant. As we examine their experiences we move from theory to practical field-tested strategies for effectively implementing change.

CASE STUDY I
Rockin' and "Rowland" in Seattle

IN A NUTSHELL

Church: Church at the Center, Seattle, Washington

Style of Worship Music: alternative/contemporary – uptempo/alternative rock

Target: non-Christian baby boomers and baby busters

Location/Community: The Seattle Center, Seattle, Washington – The church meets at the Uptown Theater, 511 Queen Anne Avenue North, just west of the Space Needle; 85 percent Caucasian, 10 percent Asian, 50 percent single, and 60 percent under age forty

Service Schedule: 9 and 10:45 a.m. (identical services)

Church Statistics: membership – 200; average attendance – worship services 330, Sunday school – 40 children, 15 adults

Pastor, Head of Staff: Randy Rowland

KEY LEARNING POINTS

A celebration-style worship service is key to reaching both the baby boomer and buster generations.

A commitment to reflect the demographic distribution of the community will often force the church into greater outreach.

When it comes to music, start slow and build on quality.

Secular, alternative rock music interfaced with the Gospel has drawn the unchurched to listen in a new way to the Gospel.

A high-tech service can have a high financial cost.

THE BIG PICTURE

Church at the Center is located in the heart of Seattle. The church was started as a "New Church Development" within the

Seattle Presbytery. Nine months later this emerging fellowship was chartered as an official church with over 100 members. Rowland epitomizes the growth and excitement of this new congregation. He says, "Our goal is to reach out to our community with a celebration-style worship service that is culturally relevant and theologically Reformed in the proclamation of the Gospel." He has committed his life to reaching the "good, happy pagans" of his generation and the generation behind them (Generation X). Church at the Center is seeing lives changed. Conversions followed by adult baptisms and reaffirmations of faith are legion and occur on a regular basis.

For some this innovative approach is too radical. Rowland responds, "We are trying to create a church that your son or daughter (who quit church) can come back to." They may see church as irrelevant to the needs of their lives. Love requires that we adapt our methods so that we can reach this generation for Christ. Rowland believes that the current challenge before the congregation is to stay on mission. If Rowland could start the church all over again, he would "be even more radical right from the start." His advice? "Start with your pioneers and let your community and church grow to it."

A VISIT TO THE CHURCH AT THE CENTER

If you do not notice the difference in the way things look, you will quickly notice a difference in the way things sound! The uptempo/alternative rock sound is strong and powerful. The exuberance is clearly felt in the clapping, loud singing, and even louder music! The service meets in a 500-seat movie theater. The music is led by a nine-piece band, usually guitar-driven alternative rock, along the lines of such rock groups as Counting Crows, REM, and U2.

The band's music is of professional quality – however, this was not always the case. Initially the band did not have a quality sound, but this did not discourage Rowland. He comments, "You must start where you are and build it slowly. The main thing is to let the little talent that you have shine. A little talent draws big talent."

Rowland is convinced that the key to the church is a musical style that is attractive and relevant. Theater lighting is used very effectively throughout the service. The words to the music are projected onto a screen with state-of-the-art graphics. Occasionally video clips introduce another avenue for the message. Drama is not a regular feature. A high-tech service is expensive. The original investment in high-tech equipment topped $60,000, and the annual payroll for worship leader and band totals about $40,000.

The Sunday morning service lasts for an hour and fifteen minutes. It's a "hands free" worship environment with no printed order of worship. The majority of the service features the newest praise and celebration music. However, each week hymns and older choruses may also be interspersed in the music. The special music is often drawn from popular, secular songs with a provocative message. Rowland thinks that most people listen to contemporary, secular music. Using this music in worship has a subliminal relevance because it connects to everyday life. If the music of the culture can be interfaced with the Gospel message, people will listen in a new way. For example, at a Christmas Eve service the band played Joan Osborne's pop hit "What If God Were One of Us?" In the sermon, Rowland compared the text of this song with the prologue to John's Gospel, showing how Christ speaks to the spiritual hunger of our lives. On another Sunday Rowland introduced his sermon on sexual temptation with a song performed by the secular rock group Crowded House. The lyrics of the song speak to giving in to temptation and the devastation that sin brings into our lives. Later in the service the band played the song, "Brains Head South" by The Basics (from their *Haven* album). The lyrics include the words, "I've been around enough to know this isn't all too clear. And it's kinda hard to think when we're already in gear. Before you flash those eyes, before I kiss your mouth, we gotta get something straight, before our brains head south."

Church at the Center helps other churches to do greater outreach to Generation X. They demonstrate that when we offer a worship service in the voice of the people without compromising the gospel, people will come with hungry hearts.

IN THEIR OWN WORDS:
RANDY ROWLAND, PASTOR, HEAD OF STAFF

Can Alternative Rock be truly Reformed?

> Rather than comparing methods of worship it is better to look at the principles that John Calvin articulated as essential in worship. Calvin believed that music is an expression of truth and beauty. The only qualification was that it should be appropriate to the Lord's day. Calvin placed no qualifications on how music had to sound. Truth and beauty are very subjective terms defined differently by different subgroups within the culture. Thus the need for a variety of worship styles. In worship we are reminded of God's presence. "God has beat you here to church." In His Sovereignty, God has uniquely set the stage for our hearts to seek Him in worship.

Is a jazz saxophone really appropriate for worship?

> Music can be played with any instrument. Singing only to the accompaniment of an organ is retrogressive. In Psalm 150 we are told to praise God with many types of instruments. There is more biblical evidence for a rock band than there is for an organ or even a choir!

CASE STUDY II
Counting the Cost – Seeking the Lost

IN A NUTSHELL

Church: First Presbyterian Church, Grand Haven, Michigan

Style of Worship Music: alternative/contemporary – uptempo/light rock

Target: Christian/unchurched, baby boomers, and baby busters

Location/Community: suburban/small town; white, highly verbal, and mostly upper-middle class

Service Schedule: 8 a.m. traditional service in the sanctuary, 9:15 a.m. contemporary worship in the fellowship hall, 11 a.m. traditional worship in the sanctuary

Church Statistics: membership 1,000; average attendance – worship services 550, Sunday school 200

Pastor, Head of Staff: Dr. Eric J. Snyder

KEY LEARNING POINTS

Integrating contemporary worship into the life of the church may be costly, but there is an even higher price to be paid if we do not. Many young families will quietly drift away to other churches that offer a worship style they perceive to be more culturally relevant.

The planning process to start a contemporary worship service should involve adequate lead time, several feedback loops, prayer, community building, and theological reflection.

The way to maintain peace, unity, and greater sense of mission at Grand Haven was the multiple-track model.

Hiring a part-time music director to lead the contemporary worship service can greatly impact the quality of the service.

Adding a contemporary service alongside two traditional services on Sunday morning can have a negative impact on the Christian Education program. Careful planning and stewardship of resources are required to deal with this problem.

Equipment needs, renovations, and salary costs can be expensive!

A key factor in the decline in the Presbyterian Church (USA) is its inability to reach baby boomers.

THE BIG PICTURE

A disturbing trend at Grand Haven had emerged. Five young couples, whose worship needs were not being met, were invited to share their concerns with the church's worship committee. They explained that their kids were not connecting with the traditional services, and as a result they were losing them to other churches or to inactivity. Several young families had already left the church. It became clear that if these concerns were not addressed in a positive way, this decline would continue.

Snyder sensed this was the opportunity for the church to respond to a need, not only within the church, but also in the community. Following his catalytic leadership, the session implemented a very thorough process that allowed time for prayer, community building, and theological reflection. This process involved four different groups totaling seventy people over a period of six months. Throughout the planning, the leadership sought feedback from the congregation. The key steps in this process involved the following:

1. An education process with worship committee and session to study the generational differences that led the younger members to express dissatisfaction.

2. Gathering of hard data reflecting worship attendance, Sunday school attendance, and giving patterns. Interviewing people who had left the church.

3. A fifteen-person task force explored the possibility of an alternative worship service. This representative task force called on several other churches that either considered or implemented contemporary worship.

4. The creation of a second task force to determine the content of the service.

5. The session decided to hire a part-time music director to lead the contemporary service. She immediately began to assemble the music team.

6. The formation of a third and final "schedule" task force. This group considered such issues as parking, where to hold the services, and how to interface with the Sunday school program.

7. Once the session had set the new policy in place, it took twelve weeks of intense work to plan the details of the service. As a result over 240 people attended the first contemporary worship service. This service continues to draw an average of 300 people per Sunday.

For this congregation an alternative contemporary worship service was better than a blend of contemporary and traditional. They came to believe that "blended worship" would only polarize and alienate. The end result of this planning process was a well-considered decision embraced by a wide majority of the church.

A VISIT TO GRAND HAVEN

The service incorporates many contemporary elements. Drama and video clips are used on occasion. A band with three vocalists leads the music. The pastoral staff takes an active role in guiding the congregation through the worship. Communion, by intinction, is offered twice a month. The service is put together on a weekly basis by a five-member team that plans and coordinates the various aspects of the service. Usually two hymns, played in a very contemporary style, are blended into the worship.

IN THEIR OWN WORDS:
ERIC J. SNYDER, PASTOR, HEAD OF STAFF

A reality check for the Presbyterian Church (USA):

> I was also aware this scenario [of losing young families] was being repeated across the country. It is well known that our denomination has declined from 4.25 million in 1966 (including the old PCUS) to 2.7 million today. Less well known is that this decline is not primarily because our members are flocking to other denominations. The decline is because we are not receiving sufficient new members to replace the 7 percent losses (1.5 percent death, 2.5 percent transfer, and 3 percent drop out) that a church experiences each year. When our denomination was growing, we were receiving 8 to 9 percent per year in new members. Now we receive about 5.7 percent per year in new members. Our problem is with intake, not with the 7 percent losses that we have experienced consistently throughout this century. Simply put, we have lost the baby boomer generation. I am persuaded that part of this has happened because we have not had openness to new worship styles.

Why blended worship will not work for every church:

> Several years ago we had an Easter service where we did a joyful, upbeat children's anthem. A particular family was greatly offended by this. As they walked out after the service they said, "If you ever do that again, my family and I will leave this church." But on the very same Sunday another family commented to me, "That was the best worship service we have ever been to and we want to join this church."

CASE STUDY III
Blooming Where You Are Planted

IN A NUTSHELL

Church: First Presbyterian Church, Mt. Holly, New Jersey

Style of Worship Music: Three distinct styles – blended, alternative/contemporary – uptempo/light rock/contemporary, traditional

Target: nonchurched baby boomers and busters

Location/Community: Mt. Holly, New Jersey; population 11,000; serving economically challenged neighborhood with an ethnically diverse population

Service Schedule: Saturday 7 p.m., Sunday 8:30, 9:45, and 11 a.m.

Church Statistics: membership 700; average attendance 500; Sunday school – 300 children, 125 adults

Pastor, Head of Staff: Jim Kraft

KEY LEARNING POINTS

Contemporary worship can help a church reach out in new ways even in a small community where there is relatively little growth.

Drama can be an important way to enhance communication and increase attendance at the service.

The building in which you hold the contemporary worship service can affect the growth potential of the service.

The synthesizer is a key instrument, especially for churches with a low budget and limited space at the front of the sanctuary.

People will attend a contemporary worship service for a variety of reasons.

THE BIG PICTURE

First Presbyterian Church, established in 1839, has all the trappings of an old, staid, mainline church. It is in a less-than-desirable location in a small town, and there are no major population centers in the county. Despite the limitations working against growth and innovation, this church has given birth to an exciting contemporary worship service that is making a difference in both the church and the community.

In 1991 the congregation decided to begin a new service, called the "Band Service," which would take place on Saturday night. A year later the Saturday service was duplicated at 9:45 on Sunday morning. The Saturday service is held at 7 p.m., the more preferred time in the community.

The Band Service grew out of the vision of the church staff. Laypeople quickly became involved and did most of the planning. During the first year, the Band Service went through several changes. Initially the goal was to provide a seeker-sensitive service. Eventually the service was redesigned to reach both the committed Christian and the seeker.

The Band Service was held in the old sanctuary. However, this soon proved to be too inflexible and small because there was no convenient place to put the band, the lighting was inadequate, and the sound quality was poor. The service was shifted to a renovated building one block away from the sanctuary. Here the pews and pulpit gave way to portable staging, movable chairs, and a backdrop made by lay members of the church. The arrangement of the room varies with the needs of the service. This change of location has had a very positive effect.

As the service continued to grow, however, other problems emerged. A song leader was needed to direct the congregational singing. The band lacked a lead guitarist, and the sound was incomplete. The Director of Music was dismissed for reasons not related to the worship. This created tensions and trust issues within the planning team. It was difficult to recruit the workers needed for the weekly setup and takedown related to the use of a multipurpose room.

The church also struggled to know how to better reach the buster generation. Associate Pastor Phil Olson comments, "We have no buster sensitivity on our worship planning team. The youngest person on our team is in his mid-thirties. Not surprisingly, there's a noticeable absence of people in the baby buster age range." Olson admits the quality of the service was affected by these problems: "People were initially attracted to our service not because it was necessarily good, but because it was different." Nevertheless, the excitement and enthusiasm of those attending the Band Service has carried it through these times of transition and adjustment.

A VISIT TO FIRST PRESBYTERIAN CHURCH

Each of the three styles of worship services has a name that reflects its unique style. The 8:30 a.m. service is called the "Praise Service" because it is a blend of contemporary and traditional praise. The 9:45 a.m. and Saturday evening services are the "Band Services" because the contemporary sound of a band dominates the services. The 11 a.m. service is referred to as the "Classic Service" because it seeks to preserve what has become valued and meaningful from the tradition of the church.

Noticeably, the Band Service does not attract a consistent constituency. The contemporary music appeals to a wide variety of people for a wide variety of reasons. While attendance has grown from 60 to 70 on Saturday and to over 100 people on Sunday, no one group stands out. Olson describes three different groups that are attracted to the service:

- Older people because of the enhanced sound.

- Those who learned English as a second language. The contemporary service, with its many graphics, use of drama and dance, is more visual and is easier to follow.

- People who have connected to the contemporary worship service because of their ethnic roots. For example, there is a regular contingent with Latin roots. They come because the music is livelier, often featuring the familiar conga drums.

IN THEIR OWN WORDS:
PHIL OLSON, ASSOCIATE PASTOR

On the importance of location:

> The building in which you choose to have your contemporary worship service can affect the growth potential of the service. The shifting to a new site was in keeping with Mt. Holly's view of enriching through choices. Growing churches will consider multiple times, styles, and locations.

On the value of using a synthesizer in worship:

> If the other volunteers in the band are not able to come to the service, the service can still have a contemporary sound because of the presence of a synthesizer. Very few clubs are now hiring a full band. Rather, they bring in a synthesizer, which can sequence the sounds needed for a particular song. A full band is very expensive and takes up space. On the other hand, a synthesizer can sequence all the other sounds and rhythm that are needed to produce contemporary worship.

The value of a planning team:

> The worship team enhances the creative process and encourages the participants to be more invested in the service. The Worship Planning Team becomes the Green Berets, who are willing to go to any effort to ensure the success of the service.

CASE STUDY IV
Small Enough for a Second Service?

IN A NUTSHELL

Church: New Covenant Presbyterian Church, Mt. Laurel, New Jersey

Style of Worship Music: contemporary service – uptempo/light rock

Target: younger adults with families, unchurched who have some previous experience with the Church

Location/Community: growing suburban bedroom community; 50 percent over age 50, 30 percent baby boomers, 20 percent age 30 and under, 100 percent Caucasian

Service Schedule: 9 a.m. contemporary worship service; 11 a.m. traditional service; Sunday school offered at both services

Church Statistics: membership – 95; average attendance – worship services 65, Sunday school 25

Pastor: Roy Langwig

KEY LEARNING POINT

A struggling church that is receiving development grant funds can add a contemporary worship service.

Sometimes "redevelopment churches" are more open to a new approach to worship because redevelopment funds are directed toward new and innovative ministries that address the decline of the church.

There are growth strategies that can be employed to counter a bad location and limited resources.

Don't wait until you have all the needed resources – an exciting vision will draw people and resources as you move forward.

Set your goals high and leave the results to the Lord. Example: We set a goal to call 12,000 people to let them know of the new service. Even though we fell short of this, 7,000 people were called. This number is far higher than many would have expected.

THE BIG PICTURE

Conventional wisdom suggests that the half-filled church is not a candidate for a second service, nor should new style be introduced since it might drive away those who do attend. Yet Roy Langwig, who had pastored New Covenant Presbyterian Church for eight years, knew that if this church was to grow, it must employ new strategies that would involve some risk. New Covenant is a "redevelopment congregation" of the West Jersey Presbytery. Growth has been difficult at New Covenant for a number of reasons. The church is in a bad location, making it inaccessible to many in the wider community. On the other hand, within a six-mile radius of the church, the community is rapidly growing. As Langwig studied the demographics of the surrounding community, he learned that at least half of their community had a preference for worship that was more contemporary. Further, several of the new members who joined New Covenant had come from churches with a contemporary worship style. The church decided to launch a new service, at a different location, to appeal to the unchurched of the community.

The seeds for the service were planted when the congregation applied for funds as a redeveloping congregation. The church agreed to pursue innovative and bold strategies for outreach. After studying the issue for three months, the session unanimously decided to start a second "alternative contemporary" service. They preferred this option because earlier attempts to have "blended worship" had not been well received. Langwig comments, "Those who preferred contemporary worship wanted us to go further with the blended style, while those who preferred more traditional became less and less tolerant with the newer music in worship."

The new service was advertised to the community primarily through a telephone campaign. Six telephone lines were temporarily installed in the church. One hundred callers were recruited, with one third of the callers coming from New Covenant and two-thirds from the presbytery. The phone campaign continued for four weeks. Those who responded positively received a follow-up phone call and three different mailings informing them of the new service.

The first service was on the first Sunday of Advent in a local school. The goal was to attract 100 people to the first service and stabilize at an average attendance of 50. The first Sunday 58 people attended, and within a few months, the average attendance had stabilized around 25. Nine months later, when it became economically unfeasible to continue renting space, the service was moved back to the church's sanctuary, where it continues. Of the people who regularly attend, 25 percent were previously inactive members of New Covenant, and 75 percent are new to the church. The service draws mostly people in their forties, with several younger families becoming regular in attendance.

A VISIT TO NEW COVENANT PRESBYTERIAN CHURCH

The service begins with a short praise chorus, which serves as a call to worship. In his opening words, Langwig focuses on one aspect of God's character that will be emphasized in the music that morning. A band composed of a keyboardist, drummer, and bass player leads the congregation in a medley of two praise choruses. A short prayer of praise is offered acknowledging God's presence. Two more songs follow this prayer. During the announcements, Langwig encourages people who have come at the last minute to feel the freedom to get up and take a brief coffee break. The people take a moment to greet one another. A praise song calls the people back together. The Scripture and message are followed by a song of response, sharing, and prayer concerns. Those present are invited to share how they see God work in their lives and in the world around them. A pastoral prayer, closing song, and benediction complete the service.

IN THEIR OWN WORDS:
ROY LANGWIG, PASTOR, NEW COVENANT CHURCH

On addressing the resistance to change in worship:

> Unwillingness to address the needs of the younger generation
> makes for a long slide toward oblivion in many smaller
> churches. It's like being a church in a changing neighbor-
> hood. Even though the ethnic group has not changed, a
> major shift is taking place. A younger generation is moving
> into the community that speaks a different musical language.
> This makes for a new cultural situation that the church must
> address.

On the feeling that smaller churches cannot do contemporary worship:

> Our experience shows that indeed it can be done. But some-
> times it will mean that we need to be more connectional with
> the presbytery and other churches in the area. We could not
> have pulled this off without the help of other congregations.
> Anyone attempting a service in a smaller congregation such
> as ours needs to make strategic alliances somewhere along the
> line. We need to overcome the thinking "If we can't do it, it
> can't be done."

Does a contemporary worship service divide a church?

> A few members felt that the church was developing a "split
> personality," but most felt this a very positive development
> for the church. The loss of being "one big family" has been
> more than out-weighed by the gain of seeing younger families
> finally coming into the church. There is now a sense of hope
> and positive expectation for the future of New Covenant
> Church.

CASE STUDY V
Spirit-Driven Contemporary Worship

IN A NUTSHELL

Church: Glendale Presbyterian Church, Glendale, California

Style of Worship Music: blended – 80 percent uptempo/light rock, 20 percent traditional

Target: builders, baby boomers, and baby busters

Location/Community: urban area just north of Los Angeles; population 200,000; affluent; 90 percent Caucasian, 5 percent Armenian, 5 percent Asian American

Service Schedule: 9 and 10:45 a.m. (both services blended worship style)

Church Statistics: membership 1,100, average attendance – worship services 850, Sunday school 350

Pastor, Head of Staff: Darrell Johnson

KEY LEARNING POINTS

Each church must find its own way to nurture peace and unity while working for renewal in worship. Glendale went from only traditional to only contemporary to multiple track to blended in its search for the right style for this community.

Truly blended worship does not just use contemporary music in one part of the service, but wherever it seems appropriate.

Glendale Presbyterian Church plays to its strength. With many in the congregation related to the film industry, video clips become prominent.

Lighting can have a major impact on the mood of the service.

Contemporary worship helps with the flow of the service.

Communion can be a time for spiritual and emotional healing.

Unity can be nurtured through a variety of feedback loops such as Sunday afternoon forums and focus groups.

THE BIG PICTURE

The worship style at Glendale Presbyterian Church has been a front-burner issue for more than a decade. The first major shift occurred when the church changed its Sunday morning worship style from two traditional services to two contemporary services. When Johnson arrived as pastor, the format was to change to an early contemporary service followed by a traditional service. Now there are two identical blended services. This approach seems to be enjoying wide acceptance.

Using two styles of worship had polarized the congregation. Johnson comments, "The congregation was being polarized by the hyper-traditionalist and the hyper-contemporary worship advocates. Both were becoming vitriolic in their insistence on what they wanted to see in the worship services." This was no longer a healthy tension. Johnson initiated congregational forums to help the congregation talk about worship-related issues. Every quarter, time was set aside on Sunday afternoon to meet with the pastor and share concerns about worship. These discussions led to a deeper understanding of worship. Johnson writes:

> The driving issue in this church is not "Should we do contemporary worship?" but rather "What is worship?" We have tried to emphasize that worship is encounter, intimacy, and enjoying the presence of God. Contemporary worship songs are only seen as a way of nurturing the congregation toward this kind of worship. The more Biblical and enriched our understanding of worship, the more we will be able to embrace many different styles.

There was a broad consensus in the middle that welcomed a more contemporary emphasis but also wanted to preserve the feeling of a traditional service. They agreed a blended style would strengthen unity. A recent survey showed that 89 percent of the church members prefer this blended approach.

A VISIT TO GLENDALE PRESBYTERIAN CHURCH

The worship style includes both traditional and contemporary. The traditional elements of the service include the reciting of creeds, the presence of a choir, the option of singing out of a hymnbook, responsive and unison readings, and a weekly bulletin including service details. Johnson believes the traditional elements greatly enrich the worship:

> There is still a large group of unchurched people who would be more comfortable searching for God in the context of a fresh, yet traditional service. An unchurched couple, with no church background, recently began attending the church. The wife is a cellist for the Pasadena Symphony. As a couple they were attracted by the high quality of music. After experiencing the worship, she commented to Pastor Johnson, "I don't know what to make of this Jesus you keep talking about. During the singing, I don't understand, but I have never experienced anything like this." After attending the church for six weeks, both the husband and the wife gave their life to Christ in an adult Sunday school class. As people are drawn to the service, they are attracted by a contagious joy in worship.

Contemporary elements include an eight-piece band, contemporary choruses, projecting video clips and the words of the songs onto a screen, drama, no robes, and no formal printed prayers.

Blended worship does not attempt to cover everything from "Bach to Rock" with equal emphasis. The music mix is decidedly more contemporary. Even the traditional elements are often styled in a contemporary way. For example, the hymns are orchestrated in a contemporary fashion. The Apostles' Creed is displayed with computer-driven graphics. Eighty to 90 percent of the music in the service is contemporary. A praise leader leads the congregation in singing and makes appropriate transitional statements from one song to the next. Johnson emphasizes that having a skilled worship leader is crucial. The praise leader enjoys the assistance of a praise team composed of soloists and choir.

Drama is used not only to set up a point in the sermon but also for announcements, preparation for prayer, and response to the sermon. A unique feature of Glendale is that at least sixty people in the congregation are either writers or producers in the film industry. They offer resources for using film clips regularly.

IN THEIR OWN WORDS:
DARRELL JOHNSON, PASTOR, HEAD OF STAFF

A slice of blended worship:

> *Crown Him with Many Crowns* is played by the organ and the synthesizer in a strong, uptempo style. The organ fades, and the synthesizer continues to play softly. As the congregation begins to recite the Apostles' Creed, a guitar joins the synthesizer. As the creed finishes, the music flows into a medley of praise choruses. The second praise chorus is based on a Psalm, so a portion of this Psalm is read responsively before the chorus is sung. The final two choruses are more reflective and encourage the worshiper to speak directly to God.

To those who complain about the noise levels, the repetition, and the intimate style:

> If the congregation goes into a chorus for the third time, you don't have to keep singing. Use that time to pray those words or to pray for the people who are being ministered to by the repetition. If you are uncomfortable with the intimacy, that's okay. Simply make a list of your needs and present them to God, but try to keep growing in your understanding of worship.

To those who prefer mainly the contemporary sound:

The Holy Spirit did not start moving in 1979. God has been active all through the centuries, and the Church has remained strong through the ages. We can't just jettison this tradition. As a father of four children, I want my kids to know the great hymns of our faith.

CASE STUDY VI
Shot Out of a Gentle Cannon

IN A NUTSHELL

Church: Menlo Park Presbyterian Church, Menlo Park, California

Style of Worship Music: 60 percent uptempo/light rock, 40 percent traditional

Target: builders, baby boomers, and busters

Location/Community: suburban, affluent, college

Service Schedule: five services – Saturday 5 and 6:30 p.m. and Sunday 8, 9:30, and 11 a.m.

Church Statistics: membership 5,000, predominantly Caucasian while attracting a significant number of Asian Americans, 80 percent college educated, 39 percent single, average attendance – worship services 3,500

Pastor, Head of Staff: Walt Gerber

KEY LEARNING POINTS

When the sanctuary is "uncomfortably full" on Sunday morning, a viable option is to add another service Saturday evening.

Menlo Park combines excellence in traditional and contemporary music in one blended service.

Recasting hymns in a more contemporary fashion has resulted in the younger generation having a greater enthusiasm for traditional hymns.

Singing from words projected on a screen has benefits even in traditional worship. A "negotiated sacrifice" on the part of the worshiper is critical in blended worship.

A benefit of blended worship is that the traditional music becomes more participative and celebrative.

Blended worship in a megachurch involves a major financial commitment.

Pastoral leadership is a major factor in nurturing a congregation toward blended worship.

THE BIG PICTURE

The worship life of the church began to move in a new direction fourteen years ago when the congregation embraced a more contemporary and participatory worship style. The leadership had noticed that many of their young people were visiting other churches in the surrounding area because they did not find the traditional worship style appealing. The church made a decision to broaden its worship style so that people from ages eight to eighty would feel that the worship was meaningful and relevant.

Moving from a church that was largely traditional to a church that is innovative and contemporary was a slow process with several key adjustments along the way. Walt Gerber's leadership style put a high priority on introducing change in a very sensitive, yet steady way. The church made adjustments when the congregation reached a comfort level. For example, one of the first innovations was to introduce more rhythm into the music, using a drum machine. This was less controversial because the sound could be adjusted and the drums did not physically appear in the sanctuary. When live drums were added over a year later, there was little controversy. Today the congregation has a high comfort level not only with drums, but also with a musician who plays other percussion instruments. When video was introduced, it was only used to project onto the screens the faces of young children who were being baptized. Later it was used for announcements related to "mission prayer points" and points being made in the sermon. Once the congregation was comfortable with these innovations, the words to the music were introduced on the video screens with little controversy.

These changes in worship have helped to make Menlo Park more attractive to young people. Now 70 percent of the members are age fifty and under, 39 percent single, and the mean age is forty. A symbol for the acceptance of contemporary elements of worship is seen when the congregation sings the song *You Turn My Mourning into Dancing*. Samba whistles have actually sounded from various parts of the congregation! The slow, gentle process has yielded dramatic changes in worship. Dry and predictable worship evolved into high-energy, high-tech, and high worship. Doug Lawrence, Minister of Music, exclaims, "The changes have been so gentle and yet so radical I feel that I have been shot out of a gentle cannon!"

A VISIT TO MENLO PARK

The design of all the services is essentially the same, differing only in the music. Each service meets in the sanctuary, a traditional Gothic design featuring stained-glass windows and large chandeliers. At the front of the sanctuary is a large platform area. Movable furnishings allow great flexibility.

The style of the worship is blended. At times a mighty electronic organ leads the singing. Other times the worship follows the beat of a pulsating band that includes a synthesizer, drums, bass, and piano. Brass, strings, and harps are added for special services. Sixty percent of the music comes from contemporary choruses, while hymns, gospel choruses, and traditional anthems remain. Occasionally the language in the hymns is changed to make it more contemporary and understandable. Lawrence notes that when the service was mainly traditional, the younger people tended to have little enthusiasm for traditional hymns. Now that the styles are more evenly mixed, younger members have responded exceptionally well to traditional hymns. Lawrence feels that when a genuine effort is made to include the younger generation, they will respond by showing a greater openness to the traditional. If they are not included, they will grow dissatisfied.

The service makes occasional use of drama. Two screens in the sanctuary allow the words to the music to be projected during singing. This has fostered more expressive singing as people sing with their heads up, rather than buried in a hymnal. Older people do need their glasses to read a bulletin. Video clips appear regularly, emphasizing points in the sermon or announcements.

IN THEIR OWN WORDS:
DOUG LAWRENCE, MINISTER OF MUSIC

On making a negotiated sacrifice:

> In order to appreciate what is offered in both the contemporary and traditional styles, the worshiper must learn to make *a negotiated sacrifice*. If this moment in worship doesn't appeal to you, pray for the person who is being blessed by this experience. When it's your turn to be blessed, that person will be praying for you. No matter what is happening in worship, we all have a job to do. Either we should be fully entering into worship or we should be praying for others who are.

On building congregational unity through a blended-worship style:

> Some day we are all going to be in heaven and experience oneness in worship. We should at least get a taste of what that is like in the here and now. This will only happen if we can experience the miracle of oneness in worship. The generation gap is wider than ever. Even within the body of Christ, people of different ages can give up on ever understanding one another. Blended worship helps us to see our inter-connectedness in the body of Christ. As seniors see the exuberance and devotion of young people loving Jesus, it softens their hearts toward the younger generation. Young people have a greater chance to benefit from the wisdom and maturity displayed by those who are older.

CASE STUDY VII
Singing a New Song from the Book of Common Worship

IN A NUTSHELL

Church: Buechel Presbyterian Church, Louisville, Kentucky

Style of Worship Music: traditional/blended

Target: people in this culturally and theologically diverse neighborhood; many prefer traditional worship forms that incorporate contemporary music in thoughtful and authentic ways.

Location/Community: urban neighborhood located in a business district; 90 percent Caucasian, 10 percent African American, 70 percent over age 50

Service Schedule: 9:15 a.m. Sunday school followed by 10:45 a.m. worship service

Church Statistics: membership 180, average attendance – worship services 105, Sunday school 45

Pastor: Megan Ritchie

KEY LEARNING POINTS

A church can follow a structured liturgy and still incorporate contemporary music into all parts of the service.

A congregation accustomed to traditional worship can experience new worship forms in authentic and nonstereotypic ways.

A theologically diverse congregation can find authentic voice in a wide variety of musical styles.

Blended worship allows the small church to use its limited resources effectively.

A broader range of music can be more readily accepted when there is a strong connection to world missions.

THE BIG PICTURE

Buechel Presbyterian Church is discovering that contemporary music and new worship forms can play a key role in renewal even when there is still a strong emphasis on traditional worship. On a typical Sunday morning most of the music is traditional, and just a quarter of it has a contemporary flavor. When Pastor Megan Ritchie came to the church, the worship style was largely Southern Traditional, and the church was in steady decline. Ritchie reflects:

> Over eighty-five percent of the congregation was over the age of fifty. Only a few children were occasionally present in the worship service. Very few teenagers attended. One of the first signs of renewal was that the youth group began to grow. As they began to attend the worship service on a more frequent basis, they shared the honest feedback that "we are bored with the music." This concern became a catalyst for change.

The church formed a task force to consider broadening the style of music to include every generation, and their survey found that most people were open to the idea. In the midst of this change, the church hired Paul Detterman as the Minister of Music. Detterman shared Pastor Ritchie's commitment to musical excellence in both contemporary and traditional music. The partnership of pastor, music staff, session, and key leaders played a key role in implementing this change.

Contemporary music was introduced in gathering songs before worship and through choral responses within the liturgy. Detterman comments:

> We make a consistent effort to avoid stereotypes and worship patterns that would unnecessarily alienate worshipers. Each week different worship styles are blended together in a way that is thoughtful, appropriate, and unpredictable. This has always been a singing church. We reach back in time as well as forward to explore the breadth of the Christian music. The

one thing we avoid like the plague is sentimentality. Through the various musical styles we are trying to incarnate the wholeness of the Gospel.

These changes in worship have facilitated renewal throughout the congregation. Some members who had stopped attending have come back to the service and sensed the change. Weekly attendance has grown, with the average growing from 85 to 105. People under age fifty account for most of the increase.

People are also participating more fully in worship. Pastor Ritchie notes that one eighty-seven-year-old woman who, as a child, was in the first picture ever taken of the church, recently told her, "I've never seen this church so alive." The trend that has heartened Pastor Ritchie the most is the growing hunger for experiencing the presence of God in worship.

Renewal in worship has led to a strong emphasis on world missions. A steady stream of missionaries visiting the denomination headquarters in Louisville attend worship at Buechel. Their presence reminds the congregation of the global Church and of the many ways to worship God.

A VISIT TO BUECHEL PRESBYTERIAN CHURCH

The service begins with brief announcements followed by a time of singing. This involves a medley of three or more choruses and hymns and serves as a call to worship. Following a strong opening hymn, the congregation is called to confession and pardon. They exchange the peace – a biblical practice that took time to develop within the congregation. Now they accept and take it quite seriously. The order outlined in the *Book of Common Worship* is the template for the service, yet worship leaders take a great deal of freedom within this form.

Detterman comments:

We explore many resources available to us at every part of the service. We try not to be rigid or predictable. Examples include singing the prayer for illumination or singing the Gospel reading with the children's choir and a soloist. Communion always uses the full Great Prayer of Thanksgiving, which is outlined in the *Book of Common Worship*.

Instruments used during the service include organ, piano, hand-bells, chimes, and tambourines. During the contemporary songs and spirituals there can be occasional clapping. The service lasts an hour and fifteen minutes.

IN THEIR OWN WORDS

The presence of God in worship both comforts and disturbs, as Paul Detterman, Minister of Music notes:

> As we have initiated changes in worship, we have tried to make the Lord Jesus Christ unavoidable. We have seen people deepen in faith and become more keenly aware of the presence of God in worship. The worship changes have become controversial for some because this has become a whole lot more church then they bargained for.

Pastor Megan Ritchie comments on dealing with the opposition to the changes in worship:

> We must work against a consumerist mentality in worship that says, "I will only worship God in my style." We work at blending the music and worship forms each week so that it will deepen our worship. Our focus should not exclusively be on what will meet my needs, but rather what it means to be faithful to God in worship.

CASE STUDY VIII
Reaching for Generation X

IN A NUTSHELL

Church: Brunswick Presbyterian Church, Troy, New York

Style of Worship Music: alternative/contemporary service with radical, ear-splitting, hard rock music

Target: baby busters and generation X

Location/Community: suburban/college

Service Schedule: Saturday 6 p.m. – Alive! @ Six, Sunday 8 a.m. – a more traditional service, 9:30 a.m. – a more contemporary service, 11 a.m. – a more traditional service

Church Statistics: membership 450, average attendance – worship services 400, Sunday school 120

Pastor, Head of Staff: Harry Heintz

KEY LEARNING POINTS

The sanctuary may have to be radically refashioned for an alternative/contemporary event aimed at Generation X.

The messages need to speak to the unique concerns of Generation X.

The format needs to have interactive communication.

The band performs the music, while the audience simply listens. In other parts of the service, it is important to find creative ways to involve the entire congregation.

A phenomenal amount of time and energy, both on the part of staff and laypeople, goes into this kind of ministry.

The band needs to be high quality.

For a congregation to effectively maintain this ministry, a core value must be "lost people matter to God."

THE BIG PICTURE

Many churches have struggled to minister to the young people of today known as Generation X – generally understood to be young people between the ages of seventeen and thirty. The leadership of Brunswick Presbyterian Church decided to tackle this problem by starting a new service called Alive! @ Six. We decided to test the waters by offering an Easter Eve service that would target Generation X. Even though this met with some success, it was clear that the church did not have the people or resources in place to keep a service like this going without a leadership team in place.

Twelve people became a planning team composed of baby boomers and baby busters. It included seekers, new Christians, and longtime members. In the early stages, the group gathered for discussion and prayer as they tried to discern what God wanted for this outreach effort. They explored needs and possibilities and considered models around the country that were effectively ministering to Generation X. They determined that the goal of the service would not be active Christian worship, but rather *pre-evangelism* in the sense that people attending would simply be invited to check out the possibility that Christianity might have something of value to say to their lives.

After several months of planning, a date was set for the first service. A public relations campaign began to explain the purpose and the plan for this service. During the month of public relations, Heintz publicly called for thirty people to make a three-month commitment to come to the service and to pray daily for God's blessings on the service. These thirty people would help boost attendance. As people came from the community to check out the service, they would sense a growing program. Further, the larger the crowd, the easier it would be for visitors to blend in and get involved at their own pace.

This planning process led to a very successful start. On the first night the space was packed. In coming weeks the program exceeded the expectations of the planning team. Over the next several months, weekly reports were given on Sunday morning about the ministry that was taking place at Alive! @ Six. Young people were encouraged to bring their friends and become a part of this exciting new ministry.

As the months progressed, it became clear that it would take a great deal of time and effort on the part of staff and volunteers to continue to maintain the service. Heintz cautions that if you are going to do outreach in innovative ways, you must be prepared to pay a heavy cost. As the service has continued, it has had difficulty drawing new people. Associate Pastor Kate Kotfila observes that the baby boomers are enthusiastic and often invite friends; however, the baby buster Christians come alone and are less willing to bring their friends to the service.

A VISIT TO ALIVE! @ SIX

The service is on Saturday night. The refashioned sanctuary looks like a theater. Banners, baptismal fonts, and hymnbooks are replaced by light trees, TV monitors, and one large screen that covers the church's stained-glass windows. The music in the service pulsates to a live band known as Lost Coin. Video forms a significant part of the service. As the band plays cutting-edge contemporary rock, TV monitors display, in MTV style, a variety of images. At times, live images of the congregation are projected onto the screen. An executive planning team composed of four to six people meets weekly to coordinate the service. Together they share responsibilities for advertising, serving as liaisons to the band, booking speakers, and arranging the special features such as video clips and dramas.

The message is communicated in a way that is varied and interactive. At the beginning of the service there is a teaser question related to the theme of the evening. Later in a section of the service called "Real Life," someone other than the speaker tells a personal story that connects to message. The talk for the evening is based on a recent current event or an issue that concerns Generation X, themes such as depression, suicide, and "McJobs and McLives." Following the message is an opportunity to ask questions. Some of the questions evoke smiles, while others are hard hitting.

IN THEIR OWN WORDS

Associate Pastor Kate Kotfila comments on the cost of ministry to Generation X:

> A phenomenal amount of time and energy goes into a ministry like this because it is so radically different from the normal way we do ministry. This ministry is difficult because the staff works with younger people who are young in their faith and lack stability. Those leading the ministry may not always follow through on assignments. Further there is a "creativity drain." Each week topics and various innovations in the service have to be creatively planned and executed. The staff has had difficulty balancing their involvement with Alive! @ Six and their many other responsibilities in the wider congregation. Each week a five-hour block of time is needed for set up and take down related to the service. There is also a very high financial cost involved with the service. About $5,000 dollars a year is set aside to fund the expenses related to Alive! @ Six.

Pastor Harry Heintz speaks of the benefits of this ministry:

> The Alive! @ Six program has clearly given our church a hearing among Generation X. But even more importantly, this ministry has galvanized the leadership of our church to be more intentional in their outreach. We have come to affirm, as a core value, that lost people matter to God and therefore they matter to us. This core value motivates us to do something radical to get a hearing with a group of people we were not reaching at all. This outreach has helped the entire church understand and reclaim the importance of outreach in all that the church does through its various ministries.

SUMMING IT ALL UP

While these case studies do not reflect an extensive survey, they do represent broad experience that can nudge our creativity and give practical insight into the many issues related to contemporary worship.

- The churches studied deployed a variety of traditional liturgical resources. All eight churches used traditional hymns on a regular basis. Three churches sang from a hymnal. The Church at the Center, incorporating a great amount of high tech and sophistication in its music, included creeds and at least two Scripture readings on a regular basis. A popular fear that the contemporary worship movement will discard the church's historic traditions did not apply to these churches.

- In each church where there was an alternative contemporary service, the pastor preached the same sermon at both the contemporary and the traditional worship services. (New Brunswick is the one exception: The sermon changed because the service was designed primarily for the seeker and not the committed Christian.) Thought-provoking, effective preaching continues to be a vital means to communicate the Good News, regardless of the worship service tempo.

- Every church studied demonstrated an increase in attendance. No church had a sudden, dramatic rise in attendance, but four churches showed a significant attendance and membership gain over a period of several years. The remaining four churches noted moderate to good growth.

- Four of the eight churches reported that having a well-rehearsed and skilled band was a very high priority and a key factor in the growth of their service.

- All eight churches followed a thorough planning process as they designed and started their new worship service or made changes in previously existing services.

- Conflict over the worship style was high in three of the eight churches. In only one did the conflict lead to a significant loss of members. Even there, membership gain exceeded loss. One factor contributing to high conflict was lack of unity between the pastor and the director of music. The degree of unity at the session level was high in each church. Emphasizing *the why* (the church's mission statement and theology) of the service rather than *the how* nurtured unity. Other assets to foster unity included establishing ways for the congregation to communicate with the leadership of the church and having a pastor who is able to build trust.

- One of the surprising findings of the study was that all the churches showed a significant commitment to ministering to social needs within the community. Understanding and caring for God's people invariably outweighed the desire for individual comfort or the imposition of individual tastes.

- Communion by intinction seemed to blend well with the contemporary style in about half the churches.

Finally, these case studies demonstrate in practical and concrete terms that contemporary worship can bring great blessing into the life and ministry of a congregation. Renewal in worship is spreading like a fire across our churches. It is my hope that from these case studies you will light your torch from this igniting flame.

Addendum
But Is It Presbyterian?

In Chapter 2 we considered the ACTS pattern for worship. Those who are familiar with the Presbyterian stream of Reformed worship should find this pattern familiar.[1] This understanding of worship is very consistent with the way worship is described in the "Directory for Worship" in the Presbyterian *Book of Order*.[2] In Section W-3.3000 entitled "Service for the Lord's Day," the basic order for Presbyterian worship is set forth as follows:

1) Gathering around the Word
2) Proclaiming the Word
3) Responding to the Word
4) The Sealing of the Word: Sacraments
5) Bearing and Following the Word into the World

The Directory for Worship (Book of Order)	Key Elements in an order of Worship
1. Gathering around the Word (W-3.3301)	
(a) Worship begins as people gather. (W-3.3301)	

(b) The people are called to worship. (W-3.3301)   **Call to Worship**

(c) Prayer or hymn of adoration is offered. (W-3.3301)   **Adoration**

(d) A prayer of confession of the reality of sin in personal and common life follows. In a declaration of pardon, the gospel is proclaimed and forgiveness is declared in the name of the Lord Jesus Christ. (W-3.3301)   **Confession**

(e) The people give glory to God (W-3.3301)   **Thanksgiving**

As the people respond to the Word, prayers of intercession are offered . . . prayers of supplication are offered.[3]   **Supplication**

The ACTS pattern for worship is more clearly spelled out in the section entitled "The Elements of Christian Worship."

In *adoration* we praise God for who God is. In *thanksgiving* we express gratitude for what God has done. In *confession* we acknowledge repentance for what we as individuals and as a people have done or left undone. In *supplication* we plead for ourselves and the gathered community. (W-2.1002, italics mine)   **ACTS**

2. Proclaiming the Word (W-3.3400)

Proclaiming God's Word

The Word shall be interpreted in a sermon preached by the preacher or in other forms authorized by the Session and by the pastor. (W-3.3400)

Suitable scripture lessons are read. (W-3.3401) Listening to the reading of the Scripture requires expectation and concentration. (W-2.2006)

Reading God's Word

3. Responding to the Word (W-3.3500)

Our Response

- Affirming and reaffirming commitments (W-3.3502). Worship should always offer opportunities to respond to Christ's call to become disciples. By professing faith, by uniting with the church, and by taking up the mission of the people of God. (W-2.5002)

Dedication

- Mission concerns (W-3.3505). Witness to faith and service and interpretation of missions and the programs of the church may be included in the service as a response to the Word. (W-3.3505)

- Prayers (W-3.3506)

- Offerings (W-3.3507). The offering

Offerings

of material goods in worship is a corporate act of self-dedication in response to God. (W-2.5003)

Baptism and the Lord's Supper

4. The Sealing of the Word: Sacraments (W-3.3600)

The Sacraments of Baptism and the Lord's Supper are God's acts of sealing the promises of faith within the community of faith as the congregation worships, and includes the responses of the faithful to the Word proclaimed and enacted in the Sacraments. (W-3.3600)

Benediction

5. Bearing and following the Word into the world (W-3.3700)

When it comes to issues in worship, "we know what we like and we like what we know." Rather than being limited to our own experience, the "Directory for Worship" offers us rich insight into worship from the Reformed perspective. From the careful study of the "Directory for Worship" we can make following general observations:

1. Reformed worship is biblical.

    The section for "The Ordering of Christian Worship" begins with these words, "Those responsible for order in Christian worship shall be faithful to the authority of the Holy Spirit speaking in and through Scripture" (W-3.1001). Appeals to tradition, preferred styles of worship, and other resources for worship are to be measured by this standard.

2. Reformed worship connects us to the Gospel and God's grace.

We acknowledge the greatness of God's character and power as we lift our voices in song and liturgy. In the prayer of confession, we are confronted by our pride and willful disobedience. We invite God to walk with us through all the joys and needs of our life as we offer prayers of petition. In the proclamation of the word, we are assured of God's forgiveness and his promise to give us a future and a hope. As we participate in the sacraments, God is present with us in a way that renews and reenergizes our faith.

3. Reformed worship draws upon our rich heritage.

Around the core values of Reformed worship we may employ a variety of styles and liturgical resources. These include "the historic experience of the Church Universal, the Reformed tradition, The Book of Confessions, the needs and the particular circumstances of the worshipping community, as well as the provisions of the form of government and this Directory." (W-1.4001)

Here are just a few of the ways the Reformed tradition can enrich our contemporary worship service: We can introduce the creeds as positive affirmations of faith. We can rearrange the great hymns of our faith in a contemporary way. (One musician describes this as "putting a fresh coat of paint on the house.") Services for Communion and Baptism will enrich the way the sacraments are observed. We can read the Scriptures as litanies in creative and thought-provoking ways.

4. Reformed worship is positive toward change and innovation.

The order of worship outlined for us in the *Book of Order* was never meant to be a hard and fast arrangement for worship:

The "Directory for Worship" is *not* a service book with *fixed orders* of worship, a collection of prayers and rituals, or a program guide. Rather it describes the theology that underlies Reformed worship and outlines appropriate forms for that worship. This Directory suggests possibilities for worship, *invites development* in worship and *encourages* continuing *reform* of worship.[4]

Our *Book of Confessions* views change in worship not only as positive but also as necessary. The Scots Confession notes, "For as ceremonies which men have devised are but temporal so they may, and *ought to be changed*."[5] Further caution is given in the *Book of Order* regarding those who would become overly concerned with the "official" order of Presbyterian worship:

> In the history of the church some have offered established forms for ordering worship in accordance with God's Word. Others, in the effort to be faithful to the Word, have resisted imposing any fixed forms upon the worshipping community. The Presbyterian Church USA acknowledges that all forms of worship are provisional and subject to *reformation*. In ordering worship, the church is to *seek openness to the creativity* of the Holy Spirit, who guides the church towards worship which is orderly, yet *spontaneous*, consistent with God's Word and open to the newness of God's future. (W-3.1002, italics mine)

This is further amplified with the words "the ordering of worship should also reflect the richness of cultural diversity in which the church ministers, as well as the local circumstances and needs of its congregation." (W-3.1003) To allow worship to reflect only the richness of one aspect of culture (i.e., "high art," best symbolized by Bach, Beethoven, and Mozart) denies the richness of our cultural diversity. Musical styles such as rock 'n' roll, jazz, rhythm and blues, alternative rock, and country western are deeply rooted in our culture. We are being good Presbyterians when our worship *reflects the richness* of these styles.

The Book of Order anticipates that, in fact, there will be many different orders of worship: "Other orders of worship may also serve the needs of a particular church and be orderly, faithful to Scripture and true to historical principles." (W-3.3202)

5. Reformed worship is contemporary.

"Beyond Scripture, no single warrant for ordering worship exists, but the worship of the church is informed and shaped by history, culture and contemporary need." (W-3-1001) As we noted in Chapter 1, the church is shaped by culture and contemporary need in that our preaching of the gospel and worship of God are expressed in the language, music, and thought forms of the culture.

NOTES

Introduction

1. Robert Wenz, *Room for God?* (Grand Rapids, MI: Baker Books, 1994), 55-56.

Chapter 1: Music to Tell the Good News

1. For an extensive treatment of how faith relates to culture, see H. Richard Neibuhr, *Christ and Culture* (New York: Harper Torch Books, 1956). He describes Christ as the transformer of culture in that "He redirects, reinvigorates, and regenerates that life of man, expressed in all human works" (ibid., 209). What distinguishes Christians is not their peculiar cultural practices, but rather the values that shape their lives. Neibuhr quotes a second-century letter to a Christian named Diogneitus to illustrate this point:

> Following the customs of the natives in respect to clothing, food and the rest of their ordinary conduct, they display to us their wonderful and confessedly striking mode of life. What makes this mode of life striking is the scorn of death, the love, meekness, and humility which have been infused into it by God through His redeeming as well as creative Word" (ibid., 205).

For Niebuhr, all culture is under God's sovereign rule and "the Christian must carry on cultural work in obedience to the Lord" (ibid., 191). By applying the values of Christ to cultural practices, the Christian transforms culture into something that can honor God.

2. Rick Warren, *The Purpose Driven Church* (Grand Rapids, MI: Zondervan Publishing House, 1995), 240.

3. For a more complete description of the baby boomer generation, see Doug Murren, *The Baby Boomerang* (Ventura, CA: Regal Books, 1990), 53.

4. Wade Clark Roof, *A Generation of Seekers: The Spiritual Journeys of the Baby Boom Generation* (San Francisco: Harper Collins, 1993), 32-60.

5. W. C. Roof and D. Roozer, as cited by Kenneth L. Woodward in "Time to Seek," *Newsweek*, 17 December 1990, 52.

6. Ibid.

7. Donald M. Brandt, *Worship and Outreach: New Services for New People* (Minneapolis: Augsburg Fortress, 1994), 13.

8. Herb Miller, "Effective Worship: Designing Services That Attract and Spiritually Enrich Contemporary Adults," Paper presented in a workshop held at Palma Sola Presbyterian Church, Bradenton, Florida, 5 October 1996, 1.

9. Ibid., 15.

10. According to recent statistics, 65 percent of unchurched people claim Christian faith is relevant to the way they live today, but only 27 percent think the Church is relevant. Though 49 percent of the unchurched say having a closer relationship with God is very desirable, only 13 percent say being part of a local church is very desirable. George Barna, *Understanding Ministry in a Changing Culture* (Glendale, CA: Barna Research Group, 1993), 90.

11. Robert E. Logan, *Beyond Church Growth* (Old Tappan, NJ: Fleming H. Revell Co., 1989), 76.

12. Miller, op. cit., 15.

13. Daniel C. Benedict and Craig Kennet Miller, *Contemporary Worship for the Twenty-first Century* (Nashville: Discipleship Resources, 1995), 120.

14. Robert Wenz, *Room for God?* (Grand Rapids, MI: Baker Books, 1994), 57.

15. Warren, op. cit., 280.

16. Ibid., 279.

17. John Calvin, *Institutes of the Christian Religion* (Grand Rapids, MI: William B. Eerdmans Publishing Company, 1972), 182.

18. As cited by Roland Bainton in *Here I Stand: A Life of Martin Luther* (New York: The New American Library, 1950), 267-269.

19. Sally Morgenthaler, *Worship Evangelism* (Grand Rapids, MI: Zondervan Publishing House, 1995), 211.

20. For the comparison of music to a disputable matter, I am indebted to Barry Liesch, *The New Worship* (Grand Rapids, MI: Baker Books, 1996), 177-188.

21. Graham Cray, "Justice, Rock, and The Renewal of Worship," *In Spirit and in Truth: Exploring Directions in Music Today*, edited by Robin Shelton (London: Hodder and Stoughton, 189), 22.

22. Liesch, op. cit., 202.

23. Michael Slaughter, *Essential Foundations for Church Renewal* (Pasadena, CA: Charles E. Fuller Institute, 1994), audiocassette.

24. Rick Warren in *The Purpose Driven Church*, (Grand Rapids, MI:

Zondervan Publishing House, 1995) 282-283, cites several examples of secular influence: John Calvin hired two secular songwriters of his day to put his theology to music; the Queen of England was so incensed by these "vulgar tunes" that she derisively referred to them as Calvin's Geneva Jogs. . . .When "Silent Night" was first published, George Webber, Music Director of the Mainz Cathedral, called it vulgar mischief and void of all religious and Christian feeling. . . . Handel's "Messiah" was widely condemned as "vulgar theater" by the churchmen of his day. Like the criticism of today's contemporary choruses, the "Messiah" was banned for having too much repetition and not enough message – it contained nearly 100 repetitions of "Hallelujah."

25. Benedict and Miller, op. cit., 11-12.

26. Dan Gilbert, "Worship with an Authentic American Character," *Worship Innovations*, (Spring 1996), 26.

27. Benedict and Miller, op. cit., 12-13.

28. Marva J. Dawn, *Reaching Out without Dumbing Down* (Grand Rapids, MI: William B. Erdmans Publishing Company, 1995), 180-181. Dawn cites this statistic and then disputes its validity. She counters that "classical music and hymnody are two different entities. Many people in the United States deeply love meaningful hymns and choose them for important occasion . . . Furthermore, what people listen to during the week on their radios does not necessarily dictate what they want in church music. In fact some people want the music of worship to be different from what they usually hear in order to remind them of the otherness of God" (loc. cit.).

29. Richard Stoll Armstrong, "Music in Service to the Gospel," *Journal of the Academy for Evangelism*, 8 (1992/93), 47.

30. Liesch, op. cit., 2.

31. Charles Arn, *How to Start a New Service* (Grand Rapids, MI: Baker Books, 1997), 20.

32. Dawn, op. cit., 149.

33. As quoted by Charles Trueheart in "The Next Church," *The Atlantic Monthly*, 278 (August 1996), 44.

34. *The Constitution of the Presbyterian Church (USA), Part II: The Book of Order* (W-1.2005 and W-1.20060).

Chapter 2: The Essentials of Worship

1. Sally Morgenthaler, *Worship Evangelism* (Grand Rapids MI: Zondervan Publishing House, 1995), 48.

2. James B. Torrance, *Worship, Community and the Triune God of Grace* (Downers Grove, IL: InterVarsity Press, 1996), 15, 22.

3. As quoted by Kenneth C. Haugk in *Christian Caregiving: A Way of Life* (Minneapolis: Augsburg, 1984), 112.

4. Perry D. LeFevre, ed., *The Prayers of Kierkegaard* (Chicago: University of Chicago Press, 1956), 21.

5. Harry E. Fosdick, "God of Grace and God of Glory," *The Worshiping Church* (Carol Stream, IL: Hope Publishing Co., 1990), 669.

6. Annie Dillard, *Teaching a Stone to Talk* (New York: Harper Perennial, 1982), 40-41.

Chapter 3: Enriching Your Worship

1. Mark Hiiva, "The Lament: When the Heart Takes Over – Psalm 42. " Worship message presented at Community Church of Joy, 16635 N 51st Street, Glendale, Arizona.

2. Gerrit Gustafson, "To Leap or To Weep," *Worship Today*, September-October 1993, 29.

3. Robert Webber, *Worship Is a Verb* (Nashville: Abbott-Martyn, 1992), 46.

4. Robert Wenz, *Room for God?* (Grand Rapids, MI: Baker Books, 1994), 77.

5. Jaroslav Pelikan, *The Vindication of Tradition* (New Haven: Yale University Press, 1984), 65.

6. Kennon Callahan, *Dynamic Worship: Mission, Grace, Praise, and Power* (San Francisco: Harper Collins, 1994), 87.

7. Keith Green, "Oh Lord, You're Beautiful" (Tampa, FL: Birdwing Music/Cherry Lane Music Publishing Co., Inc., 1980).

8. Ronald Scates, "Why They Come, Why They Stay," *Reformed Worship*, March 1996, 11-13.

9. Robert Webber, "Three Principles That Make Worship Christian," *Worship Leader*, April-May 1992, 6.

10. Drawn from notes taken by Sally Morgenthaler at the Willow Creek Church Leadership Conference, October 1990.

11. Sally Morgenthaler, *Worship Evangelism* (Grand Rapids, MI:

Zondervan Publishing House, 1995), 23, 24.

12. Wenz, op. cit., 29.

Chapter 4: Designing Your Contemporary Worship Service

1. Herb Miller, "Net Results!" *New Ideas in Church Vitality and Leadership* (September 1995), 4, 5.

2. Charles Trueheart, "The Next Church," *Atlantic Monthly* 278 (August 1996), 37.

3. Gary McIntosh suggests this in *The McIntosh Church Growth Network Newsletter*, October 1995, 2.

4. George Barna, *Never on a Sunday: The Challenge of the Unchurched* (Glendale, CA: Barna Research Group, 1990), 30.

5. George Barna, "The Dream Church," *Ministry Currents*, April-June 1992, 3.

6. Daniel C. Benedict and Craig Kennet Miller, *Contemporary Worship for the Twenty-first Century* (Nashville: Discipleship Resources, 1995), 25.

7. Marva J. Dawn, *Reaching Out without Dumbing Down* (Grand Rapids, MI: William B. Eerdmans Publishing Company, 1995), 177. In passing it should be noted that this congregation division along age lines only proves the point that contemporary worship is preferred by the younger generation – a point that Dawn elsewhere seems to dispute.

8. According to Herb Miller, 70 percent of all baby boomers prefer the contemporary worship style. "Effective Worship: Designing

Services That Attract and Spiritually Enrich Contemporary Adults,"
Paper presented in a workshop held at Palma Sola Presbyterian
Church, Bradenton, FL, 5 October 1996, 17.

9. Marva J. Dawn, op. cit., 177.

10. Ibid.

11. Sally Morgenthaler, *Worship Evangelism* (Grand Rapids, MI:
Zondervan Publishing House, 1995), 243.

12. Bob Gilliam, cited by Bill Hull in *Power Religion: The Selling Out
of the American Church*, Michael Scott Horton, ed. (Chicago: Moody
Bible Press, 1992), 143.

13. Joe Maxwell, "Whatever Happened to Evangelism?" *Charisma
and Christian Life*, December 1993, 14.

14. This point is readily conceded by the leadership of Willow Creek
Community Church. Charles Arn comments, "Rev. Bill Hybels, pastor of Willow Creek Community Church (South Barrington, Illinois)
– the church widely associated with popularizing the term seeker
service – does not use the word worship to describe the church's
weekend services. The word is reserved for the midweek service for
believers." Charles Arn, *How to Start a New Service*, 102.

Chapter 5: Starting a Contemporary Service – A Twenty-Point Checklist

1. The chart I am presenting here is an adaptation of the chart presented by Charles Arn in *How to Start a New Service* (Grand Rapids,
MI: Baker Books, 1997), 91-116. Arn's thought related to targeting
groups has been influential in the following discussion related to
identifying those you are seeking to reach. For an expanded version

of this brief discussion and a more concise definition of the terms "seniors," "boomers," and "busters" and how these three groups relate to worship, see Arn, op. cit., 93-100.

2. Cheryl Hayner, *Contemporary Worship Survey Results* (Madison, WI: unpublished survey, 1997), 2.

3. Charles Arn, *How to Start a New Service* (Grand Rapids, MI: Baker Books, 1997), 135.

Addendum: But Is It Presbyterian?

1. If the reader is unfamiliar with the concept of "Reformed worship," a helpful starting point is found in the three often-cited slogans of the Reformation – *sola scriptura* (scripture alone), *sola fides* (faith alone), and *sola gratia* (grace alone). *Sola scriptura* anchors our worship, not to changing human traditions, but to the biblical pattern for worship. *Sola Fides* informs us that God requires sincere faith and not mere outward conformity to a liturgical form. *Sola gratia* reminds us that even our inclination to faith and worship comes from God. It is grace alone that draws us and continues to sustain us despite our own unfaithfulness. The "Directory for Worship" uses the phrase "Reformed worship" to describe the theology that should regulate worship in Presbyterian churches.

2. *The Constitution of the Presbyterian Church (U.S.A.), Part II: The Book of Order* (W-3.3000). Hereafter I will refer to *The Book of Order* by indicating the letters that reference it by paragraph.

3. Even though these prayers come after the sermon, they are listed as key elements of the service. I have placed them here so that the ACTS pattern can be observed (see Section W-3.3506).

4. Preface to *The Constitution of the Presbyterian Church (USA), Part II:*

The Book of Order, "Directory for Worship," Paragraph "a" (italics mine).

5. *The Constitution of the Presbyterian Church (USA), Part I: The Book of Confessions,* 3.21, (italics mine).

SELECTED BIBLIOGRAPHY

Armstrong, Richard Stoll. "Music in Service to the Gospel," *Journal of the Academy for Evangelism.* 8 (1992/93).

Arn, Charles. *How to Start a New Service.* Grand Rapids, MI: Baker Books, 1997.

Barna, George. *Understanding Ministry in a Changing Culture.* Glendale, CA: Barna Research Group, 1993.

Benedict, Daniel C. and Craig Kennet Miller. *Contemporary Worship for the Twenty-first Century.* Nashville: Discipleship Resources, 1995.

Brandt, Donald M. *Worship and Outreach: New Services For New People.* Minneapolis: Augsburg Fortress, 1994.

Callahan, Kennon L. *Dynamic Worship.* San Francisco: Harper Collins, 1994.

Constitution of the Presbyterian Church (USA), The, Part I: Book of Confessions. Louisville: Geneva Press, 1991.

Constitution of the Presbyterian Church (USA), The, Part II: Book of Order, "Directory for Worship." Louisville: Geneva Press, 1995.

Dawn, Marva J. *Reaching Out without Dumbing Down.* Grand Rapids, MI: William B. Eerdmans Publishing Co., 1995.

Dobson, Ed. *Starting a Seeker Sensitive Service.* Grand Rapids, MI: Zondervan Publishing House, 1993.

Frame, John M. *Contemporary Worship Music: A Biblical Defense.* Phillipsburg, NJ: Presbyterian and Reformed Publishing Company, 1997.

Hayford, Jack. *Worship His Majesty.* Waco, TX: Word, 1987.

Hayford, Jack, John Killinger, and Howard Stevenson. *Mastering Worship.* Portland: Multnomah, 1990.

Hoge, Dean R., Benton Johnson, and Donald A. Luidens. *Vanishing Boundaries: The Religion of Mainline Protestant Baby Boomers.* Atlanta: Westminister/John Knox Press, 1994.

Keifert, Patrick R. *Welcoming the Stranger. A Public Theology of Worship and Evangelism.* Grand Rapids, MI: Fortress, 1992.

Liesch, Barry. *The New Worship.* Grand Rapids, MI: Baker Books, 1996.

Logan, Robert E. *Beyond Church Growth.* Old Tappan, NJ: Fleming H. Revell Co., 1989.

Martin, Ralph P. *The Worship of God.* Grand Rapids, MI: William B. Eerdmans Publishing Co., 1982.

Miller, Craig Kennet. *Baby Boomer Spirituality.* Nashville: Discipleship Resources, 1992.

Miller, Herb. "Effective Worship – Designing Services That Attract and Spiritually Enrich Contemporary Adults." Paper presented in a workshop held at Palma Sola Presbyterian Church, Bradenton, FL, 5 October 1996.

Morgenthaler, Sally. *Worship Evangelism.* Grand Rapids, MI: Zondervan, 1995.

Murren, Doug. *The Baby Boomerang.* Ventura, CA: Regal Books, 1990.

Old, Hughes O. *Guides to the Reformed Tradition: Worship*. Atlanta: John Knox Press, 1984.

Pritchard, Gregory A. *The Willow Creek Seeker Service*. Grand Rapids, MI: Baker Books, 1996.

Roof, Wade Clark. *A Generation of Seekers: The Spiritual Journeys of the Baby Boom Generation*. San Francisco: Harper Collins, 1993.

Sorge, Bob. *Exploring Worship*. Canandaigua, NY: Bob Sorge, 1987.

Torrance James B. *Worship, Community and the Triune God of Grace*. Downers Grove, IL: InterVarsity Press, 1996.

Towns, Elmer. *Putting an End to the Worship Wars*. Nashville: Broadman and Holman Publishers, 1997.

Tozer, A. W. *The Pursuit of God*. Camp Hill, PA: Christian Publications, 1982.

Trueheart, Charles, "The Next Church," *Atlantic Monthly*, August 1996.

Wardle, Terry. *Exalt Him! Designing Dynamic Worship Services*. Camp Hill, PA: Christian Publications, 1989.

Warren, Rick. *The Purpose Driven Church*. Grand Rapids, MI: Zondervan Publishing House, 1995.

Webber, Robert E. *Signs of Wonder. The Convergence of Liturgical and Charismatic Worship*. Nashville: Abbott-Martyn, 1991.

_____. *Worship Is a Verb*. Nashville: Abbott-Martyn, 1992.

Wenz, Robert. *Room for God? A Worship Challenge for Church Growth and a Marketing Era.* Grand Rapids, MI: Baker, 1994.

Woodward, Kenneth L. "A Time to Seek," *Newsweek*, December 17, 1990.

Wright, Timothy. *A Community of Joy.* Nashville: Abingdon Press, 1994.

RESOURCES FOR CONTEMPORARY WORSHIP

Praise Chorus Book. Laguna Hills, CA.: Maranatha Music, 1983, 1990.

Songs for the Congregation. Laguna Hills, CA.: Maranatha Music, 1991.

Songs for Praise and Worship: Singalong Edition. Waco, TX: Word Music, 1992.

Willow Creek Drama Resources
Zondervan Publishing
(800) 253-4475
Contemporary skits that work well in a variety of settings

Christian Copyright Licensing, Inc.
(800) 234-2446
The annual congregational fee is based on the average Sunday morning worship attendance.

Precept (formerly Church and Development Services)
(800) 442-6277
Demographic information on any area in the United States

Integrity Music, Inc.
P.O. Box 16813
Mobile, AL 36616
(205) 633-9000

Maranatha Music
P.O. Box 31050
Laguna Hills, CA 92654
(800) 245-7664

Word Music
5221 N. O'Connor Blvd., Ste 1000
Irving, TX 75039
(615) 385-9673